"IT MUST BE HERE SOMEWHERE—LOOK UNDER THE
TABLE."

The Mystery at Lilac Inn.   *Page* 37

"I DIDN'T EXPECT TO MEET YOU HERE," NANCY SAID
GRACIOUSLY.

The Mystery at Lilac Inn. Page 76

NANCY SAW SOMETHING WHITE FLUTTER FROM HIS
POCKET.

The Mystery at Lilac Inn.   *Page* 122

"THOUGHT YOU'D BE SMART, DIDN'T YOU!" SHE SNEERED.

The Mystery at Lilac Inn.　　　　　　　　　*Frontispiece (Page* 163)

NANCY DREW MYSTERY STORIES

THE MYSTERY AT LILAC INN

BY

CAROLYN KEENE

AUTHOR OF "THE SECRET OF THE OLD CLOCK,"
"THE HIDDEN STAIRCASE," ETC.

ILLUSTRATED BY
RUSSELL H. TANDY

WITH AN INTRODUCTION BY
MILDRED WIRT BENSON

FACSIMILE EDITION

BEDFORD, MASSACHUSETTS
APPLEWOOD BOOKS

For further information about these editions, please write:
Applewood Books, Box 365, Bedford, MA 01730.

LIBRARY OF CONGRESS CATALOGING-IN-PUBLICATION DATA
Keene, Carolyn.
    The mystery at lilac inn / by Carolyn Keene; illustrat-
ed by Russell H. Tandy; with an introduction by Mildred
Wirt Benson. —Facsimile ed.
        p.   cm.   — (Nancy Drew mystery stories)
    Summary: Teenage detective Nancy Drew finds herself
in danger when she sets out to track a jewel thief.
    ISBN 1-55709-158-7
    [1. Mystery and detective stories.]   I. Tandy, Russell
H., ill.   II. Title.   III. Series: Keene, Carolyn. Nancy Drew
mystery stories.
PZ7.K23Myc   1994
[Fic]–dc20   94-9297
                                                CIP
                                                AC

10 9 8 7 6

PUBLISHER'S NOTE

Much has changed in America since the Nancy Drew series first began in 1930. The modern reader may be delighted with the warmth and exactness of the language, the wholesome innocence of the characters, their engagement with the natural world, or the nonstop action without the use of violence; but just as well, the modern reader may be extremely uncomfortable with the racial and social stereotyping, the roles women play in these books, or the use of phrases or situations which may conjure up some response in the modern reader that was not felt by the reader of the times.

For good or bad, we Americans have changed quite a bit since these books were first issued. Many readers will remember these editions with great affection and will be delighted with their return; others will wonder why we just don't let them disappear. These books are part of our heritage. They are a window on our real past. For that reason, except for the addition of this note and the introduction by Mildred Wirt Benson, we are presenting *The Mystery at Lilac Inn* unedited and unchanged from its first edition.

THE NANCY I KNEW

By
MILDRED WIRT BENSON

AUTHOR OF
PENNY PARKER MYSTERY STORIES
DANGEROUS DEADLINE;
TWIN RING MYSTERY; QUARRY GHOST,
AND OTHERS

MOST FICTIONAL characters quickly are forgotten, even by their authors.

From the outset, Nancy Drew was different. She began as an unassuming, bare-bones name supplied by a syndicate, then almost in an instant, exploded into a vibrant ball of energy, unfettered, eternally seeking adventure and challenge.

Possibly it was this quality, combined with a stubborn determination to survive against all odds, that endeared her to readers. Never patterned after a real person, the character projected a dream image, one with which readers of diverse age and motivation readily could identify.

The Secret of the Old Clock, the first volume in the long-running Nancy Drew mystery series, was written by me for the Stratemeyer Syndicate, then of New York City, in 1929, with the publication date of 1930. Two years earlier, as a University of Iowa graduate student, I had authored volumes of the Ruth Fielding series, which featured a young woman carving a career in the moving picture industry. In these early stories, I carried on a main character that had been established by other syndicate writers.

Edward Stratemeyer, a prolific writer of series books, and owner of the syndicate bearing his name, wrote me that he hoped to launch a new mystery series for girls. Would I undertake it?

He then sent me a brief, unchaptered outline and the book title. His instructions were to end each chapter with cliff-hanging suspense, and to include several paragraphs promoting other proposed books in the series. Otherwise, I was on my own.

Though the series was launched more than sixty years ago, I still recall sitting at my battered old typewriter, staring at a blank sheet of paper. The plot was a familiar one, centering around a hidden will. Nancy existed in name only, without purpose or personality.

I typed a sentence or two, and threw them away. Then full-blown, a paragraph flashed into my mind:

"It would be a shame if all that money went to the Tophams! They will fly higher than ever."

Self-assured, ready at the drop of a typewriter

key to help the downtrodden by righting a wrong, Nancy herself had spoken.

At that moment, we were as one, a satisfying association which endured nearly 30 years until it became the responsibility of others to carry on her exploits and aspirations.

Dramatic changes soon came to the world, especially in communication, transportation and the attitude of people. Through it all, Nancy, as I envisioned her, stood rock-firm, untouched by war, the Depression, economic or moral problems—a trustworthy symbol for parents and children.

Before World War I, the tiny Iowa town of Ladora, where I was born, had no public libraries and few books.

Our own family library, more extensive than most, featured volumes of history, sets of the classics, and medical books which belonged to my father, the community's only doctor.

Whenever I could, I borrowed books from neighbors, reading everything available without discrimination. Stories for children were exceedingly rare.

The Tale of Peter Rabbit by Beatrix Potter fell into my hands at an early age. I read it from cover to cover. Then, because it had to be returned to the owner, I made my own handwritten copy. The result was a bitter disappointment. My scribbling was illegible. Though my parents were financially secure, it did not occur to them to buy me a published copy.

Fortunately, the lack of reading matter changed for the better one summer when the family spent two weeks in Chicago, where my father updated his surgical skills at Cook County Hospital.

Quickly I discovered the public library. Day after day, from early morning until the dinner hour, while my parents went about their affairs, I lived in the public reading room. Coming upon a shelf of fairy stories, I read each wonderful book as fast as I could. My first vacation was nearly over before I realized that many of the tales were repeats or imitations of the others.

As I grew older, Louisa May Alcott's *Little Women* came into my possession. How I loved the forthright character of Jo, at odds with so many of the day's domestic-type fictional heroines.

In general, I preferred boys' books to those written for girls. I raced through many of the Horatio Alger books because they were everywhere, the Rover Boys, and a few of the popular Ruth Fielding stories, never dreaming I would be asked to write this series in later years.

The town's high school library consisted of a single glass case filled mostly with dusty textbooks and a complete set of Dickens, through which I struggled laboriously. I craved to read, but the available literature neither challenged nor satisfied me.

Magazines in part filled the void. *St. Nicholas*, a monthly, was my favorite. I devoured every page, but mystery serials by Augusta H. Seaman, and a series of career articles devoted to men who accomplished unusual things in the work world, especially appealed to me. The magazine also sponsored children's writing contests, stirring me to compete. My first short story eventually won a silver badge, and thereafter, through my school days, I gained experience by writing children's sports stories for various church publications.

My first book, *Ruth Fielding and Her Great Scenario,* written in 1926 for Mr. Stratemeyer, was typical of assignments which followed. From a two-and-a-half-page plot, I turned out a 25-chapter, 210-page story loaded with suspense.

The brevity of the plot and the need to fill space gave me ample opportunity to invent my own scenes and to build up the main character. However, I knew nothing of the emerging moving picture industry, and needed to look up the meaning of the word "scenario" in the dictionary before agreeing to write the book.

When confronted with unfamiliar subject matter, it was my custom to load up on background material, absorbing it rapidly. Often I became so interested in a described sport or topic that I would delve deeper after the story was finished. This was especially true with such subjects as aviation, boating, and horseback riding.

The Mystery at Lilac Inn, the fourth volume in the Nancy Drew series, was written during a time of syndicate ownership transition, and so may be of special interest to book collectors.

Unfortunately, the spectacular success of the series' initial three volumes had been followed by the unexpected death, in 1930, of Mr. Stratemeyer. Without previous experience, his daughters, Harriet Adams and Edna Squier, took over the business, carrying it on without interruption. At the suggestion of the publisher, I was asked to keep on writing the Nancy stories.

As usual, a working plot was sent. This one presented technical problems. Overnight, Nancy became more of a home-type person, in early chapters focusing upon household responsibilities.

In Chapters Five and Six, a jewel theft occurs at Lilac Inn, but strangely, Nancy isn't there. Critics apparently never noticed, possibly because in later chapters, the sleuth more than makes up for her absence by going all out to catch the thieves.

In Chapter 18, an eerie atmosphere initiates the action:

"Nancy Drew was by nature a brave girl, but as she glanced at the leaden sky, she was more than a little disturbed. Almost in an instant it had become dark and the blackness seemed to have a terrifying quality. The air was warm and heavy. An oppressive quiet was broken only by the moan and rush of the river.

"Suddenly there was a vivid flash of lightning, followed by a violent clap of thunder. The clouds seemed to open wide, pouring out a torrent of rain."

The storm kept on, and so did Nancy, who rashly enters an old house alone, is captured, and winds up a prisoner in the cabin of a motorboat, speeding down river.

In her predicament, Nancy was unable to feel the driving rain and wind, and so was compelled to imagine everything that went on topside. Storms were an integral part of most early syndicate plots—loved by me as space fillers. However, this one was a real challenge.

Lilac Inn marked minor changes in writing style and in Nancy's character. The syndicate's new owner asked that I make the sleuth less bold and that abrupt sentence endings be avoided. In editing, a simple, "Nancy said" became "Nancy said sweetly," "she said kindly," and the like, all designed to produce a less abrasive, more caring type of character.

Despite suggestions, Nancy stubbornly remained herself, and judging from reader letters, she never was offensive. In the 1950s and later, all books in the series were rewritten by other syndicate authors who retained few if any of the original scenes.

Nancy, as I knew her, was on the verge of disappearing forever from print. Fortunately, she has been rescued from oblivion, and in the Applewood Books editions, remains unchanged.

Problems confronting young people today are entirely different than when I wrote *Lilac Inn*. Nevertheless, were I to re-create the character, I feel certain I would make her the same carefree, morally sound, well-adjusted individual, able to cope with whatever came her way.

So, I find it especially gratifying to examine the new editions, which in a remarkable way duplicate not only the text, but the jacket covers, the fine Russell H. Tandy illustrations and make-up of the initial stories. Side by side, an author's copy and the Applewood version appear almost identical.

Girls today, I think, will find the tales as intriguing as did their mothers and grandparents. Hopefully, generations of readers will remember Nancy's philosophy and values long after her exciting adventures have been forgotten.

NANCY DREW MYSTERY STORIES

THE MYSTERY AT LILAC INN

BY

CAROLYN KEENE

AUTHOR OF "THE SECRET OF THE OLD CLOCK,"
"THE HIDDEN STAIRCASE," ETC.

ILLUSTRATED BY
RUSSELL H. TANDY

NEW YORK
GROSSET & DUNLAP
PUBLISHERS

Made in the United States of America

NANCY DREW
MYSTERY STORIES

BY

CAROLYN KEENE

12mo. Cloth. Illustrated.

THE SECRET OF THE OLD CLOCK

THE HIDDEN STAIRCASE

THE BUNGALOW MYSTERY

THE MYSTERY AT LILAC INN

GROSSET & DUNLAP, PUBLISHERS, NEW YORK

The Mystery at Lilac Inn

CONTENTS

CHAPTER		PAGE
I	A CHANCE MEETING	1
II	RISING TO AN OCCASION	10
III	A QUEER GIRL	17
IV	ABOUT THE CRANDALL JEWELS	24
V	AT LILAC INN	31
VI	ACCUSATIONS	38
VII	DAMAGING RUMORS	45
VIII	MRS. WILLOUGHBY'S CALL	52
IX	NANCY INVESTIGATES	61
X	AN ENCOUNTER	70
XI	A TRIP TO THE INN	80
XII	A NEW DISCOVERY	87
XIII	A SURPRISE	96
XIV	NEW INFORMATION	103
XV	WHAT MR. DREW LEARNED	111
XVI	THE STRANGER	121
XVII	A CRISIS	129
XVIII	DURING THE STORM	137

iv   Contents

CHAPTER   PAGE
   XIX   IN THE STOREROOM 146
    XX   A PRISONER 154
   XXI   DOWN THE RIVER 161
  XXII   SINKING 170
 XXIII   CAPTURED 177
  XXIV   THE SEARCH 185
   XXV   NANCY'S REWARD 192

THE MYSTERY AT
LILAC INN

CHAPTER I

A CHANCE MEETING

A BRIGHT blue roadster, low-swung and smart, rolled swiftly along the winding lake road to halt suddenly before a large signboard which boldly proclaimed to all who chanced that way:

LILAC INN: CHICKEN DINNERS
OUR SPECIALTY.

The driver, a pretty girl of perhaps sixteen, attractive in a frock which either by accident or design exactly matched the blue of the automobile, smiled whimsically as she read the words.

"My specialty, too!" Nancy Drew told herself. "The thought of chicken almost makes me expire from hunger. I think I'll stop here for luncheon"

Guiding the car into the side road, she drove beneath a long canopy of trees and presently came within sight of Lilac Inn. As she swung the roadster into line with the row of automobiles parked in the yard, it seemed to her that the old inn had never appeared more picturesque than on this particular spring day. Huge lilac bushes, heavy with bloom, completely surrounded the rambling structure, while a well-kept lawn sloped gently to a crystal lake at the rear.

Alighting from the roadster, Nancy stood for a moment gazing toward the lake. So absorbed was she in the beauty of the scene that she failed to notice the approach of a girl who from appearance might have been her own age.

"Nancy Drew of all people!" the stranger cried eagerly as she rushed up.

Startled at hearing her name called, Nancy Drew wheeled quickly and then smiled as she recognized a former classmate whom she had not seen for many weeks. It was not difficult to smile upon Emily Crandall, for her candid blue eyes, delicate coloring, and almost classical features gave her a beauty which was the envy of her friends. Though she lacked Nancy Drew's poise and keen mind, she did possess an unusually sunny disposition and had a way of accepting life as she found it.

Since the death of her mother many years

before, she had been under the guardianship of Mrs. Jane Willoughby, a young widow. Unfortunately, Emily Crandall had never had a great deal of money; but the lack of it did not appear to trouble her.

"Emily Crandall!" Nancy exclaimed in genuine delight, gripping her friend's hand. "What brought you here?"

"Oh, I was driving to River Heights to see a friend. Mrs. Willoughby lent me her sedan for the day; but, as luck would have it, the mean thing stalled. I walked here thinking I might find someone to help me."

"Perhaps you're only out of gasoline."

"I'm afraid not. But why worry about such a trifle as a stalled car? After all, it was fortunate that I was forced to stop here; otherwise I should have missed you. What are you doing here, anyway? Looking for another mystery?"

"I should say not!" Nancy Drew returned emphatically. "I think I've had enough of mystery to last me a life time. Anyway, if I were looking for one, I wouldn't choose such a lovely spot as Lilac Inn."

"Mysteries sometimes pop up in strange places, Nancy, and I must say you have a faculty for running into them. Everyone said it was a wonderful piece of detective work when you solved the mystery of the Jacob Aborn bungalow. I read glowing accounts of your cleverness in the papers. Just imagine capturing a criminal! I'd be thrilled to death!"

"I was glad to help Laura Pendleton regain her inheritance," Nancy said quietly. "But I'm afraid the reporters exaggerated my part a little." Then to change the subject: "Have you had luncheon?"

"No, I haven't, and it's after one o'clock, too. I'm nearly starved."

"Then why not lunch with me? After that, we can see what can be done about your car."

"Suits me," Emily agreed willingly.

Arm in arm the two girls hurried up the path to the inn. Entering, they saw that the dining room was crowded, but the head waiter bowed to Nancy in recognition, and, to the astonishment of persons who had not received choice tables, they were promptly escorted to a secluded nook which permitted an excellent view of the lake and the grounds.

"How do you do it?" Emily asked in a low tone when the girls were seated. "The waiter gave us the very nicest table in the room."

"Oh, I've been here before. That probably explains it."

"You know it doesn't, Nancy Drew; but you're too modest to admit that you're something of a personage. At the rate you're going, you'll soon be as famous as your father."

"Oh, Emily!" Nancy protested. "What possesses you, anyway? Just because I've solved a few old mysteries—" her voice trailed off as she studied the menu card. "I can't make up my mind what to order."

"You're positively the limit," Emily sighed, as she too turned her attention to the bill of fare. "Food interests you more than an honest compliment."

"Right now I'm afraid I must admit it does," Nancy laughed. "You see, I've driven nearly seventy miles since breakfast. Dad sent me over to Windlow with some legal papers for Judge Howell. I started back without luncheon."

"I'm glad you did, Nancy. Otherwise we'd not have met here."

Nancy Drew finished writing out her order, and after handing it to the waiter settled back in her chair.

"Tell me what you have been doing with yourself this summer, Emily. I haven't seen you for ages."

"Can't you guess by looking at my freckles? I've been living at a cottage on the lake."

"Alone?"

"Oh, no! With Mrs. Willoughby. She's a dear, Nancy, but she's not to be my guardian much longer."

"Why, how is that?" Nancy inquired in surprise.

"Well, in less than a week I'll be of age. I'll be eighteen next Friday. And it's going to be the most exciting birthday I ever had!"

"You mean because you'll be free from your guardian?"

"Oh, no. I always liked Mrs. Willoughby. I'm thrilled because I'm to come into my inheritance."

"Your   inheritance?   Why,   I   didn't know——"

"Neither did I until last week," Emily broke in. "There was very little left of my mother's estate, but it seems that by my grandmother's will I'm to come into the Crandall family jewels."

"Oh, Emily, how wonderful! I've always heard of the famous Crandall jewels."

"They're   beauties,   Nancy—mostly   diamonds, too. Valued at not a cent less than forty thousand dollars."

"I'd love to see them."

"Well, you shall. Mrs. Willoughby is to turn them over to me on Friday."

"Doesn't it worry you, Emily? I wouldn't know how to take care of such an inheritance."

"Well, it does worry me a little," Emily admitted slowly. "But of course I'll rent a safety deposit box at the bank."

"I wouldn't delay if I were you."

"I guess I won't," Emily decided, after a moment of thought. "I've been in a state of respectable poverty too long to risk losing my fortune now that I've come into it. However, I won't dispose of the jewels until after you've seen them, Nancy. Can't you motor out to our cottage next Friday?"

"Of course I'll come," Nancy returned eagerly. "I wouldn't miss an opportunity to see the Crandall jewels."

By this time the waiter had appeared, bearing a tray of food, and the girls turned their attention to the good things which were placed before them.

"You haven't told me a thing about yourself," Emily presently said to her friend. "I guess I've been monopolizing the conversation."

"Oh, there's nothing special to tell. Last summer I had a thrilling time of it at Melrose Lake, but this year I'm afraid I'll be stuck in River Heights all summer unless I can find a new housekeeper to take Hannah Gruen's place."

"Your servant is leaving?"

"Yes. Her sister is ill, and she's expecting to be called away any day now to take care of her. I dread looking for another to take her place. You don't know where I can find a good housekeeper, do you?"

"Indeed I don't. I'm afraid you'll have quite a time finding anyone."

"I don't doubt it," Nancy sighed. "But at least I'll have several days before Hannah leaves. That will give me a chance to break in a new girl."

The two finished their luncheon, and although Emily protested, Nancy insisted on paying the check. They left the dining room, pausing outside the door.

"If you'll excuse me for a minute, I'll make a telephone call," Nancy said. "I must let Dad know that I'll be late in reaching River Heights, or he'll be worried."

Hurrying away, she sought a telephone booth and quickly put in a call to River Heights. After a brief wait, she heard her father's voice at the other end of the wire.

"Hello, Nancy," Carson Drew began before she could say a word. "Jove! I'm glad you called just now. I've been trying to reach you for the last two hours."

"Why, what has happened?" Nancy demanded in alarm.

"I just received a telegram from Judge Graham—you know, he's one of the biggest men in the state. He'll spend the coming week-end with us."

"Oh!" Nancy gasped, but instantly arose to the occasion. "Well, I guess we can manage it all right. I'll come home just as quickly as I can."

"I haven't told you the worst, Nancy! Hannah just learned that her sister has suffered a relapse. She's planning to leave on the three-twenty train."

"Leaving to-day?"

"Yes, with Judge Graham coming! You must get busy at once."

"I'll rush right home, Dad, and see what can be done. But I'm dreadfully afraid it will be impossible to find anyone to take her place on such short notice."

"Do the best you can, Nancy. I'm depending upon you."

With that, Carson Drew said good-by and hung up the receiver.

Nancy Drew stood for a moment staring blankly at the telephone. She knew that her father, being a man, had no comprehension of the Herculean task which lay before her. In some way she must find a satisfactory housekeeper before Judge Graham's arrival, but how it was to be accomplished she did not know.

CHAPTER II

RISING TO AN OCCASION

LEAVING the telephone booth, Nancy Drew hurried back to where she had left Emily Crandall and quickly explained that she must start at once for River Heights.

"Can't I drop you off at the nearest garage?" she offered. "You can find a mechanic and go back after your car."

"Won't it be out of your way?"

"Not at all. There's a garage about three miles from here."

"Then I'll certainly accept your offer, because I don't want to camp on the road all day."

Nancy led the way to the roadster. Skillfully turning in the narrow parking space, she drove down the lane to the main road and soon left Lilac Inn far behind. Presently sighting a roadside garage, she stopped the car and Emily alighted.

"Don't forget you're to see the Crandall jewels next Friday," she reminded Nancy as she said good-by.

"I won't."

As Emily stepped back, Nancy shifted gears. The roadster moved slowly away, and then gathered speed. Nancy Drew drove rapidly, for she was eager to reach home, knowing that much work was awaiting her. She glanced at her watch and saw that it was after two o'clock. She must hurry if she was to get there before Hannah left.

It was exactly two-thirty when she reached the outskirts of River Heights. Following the boulevard, she came within sight of her own home and was relieved to see her father's automobile standing at the door. That meant that he had not yet taken Hannah to the railroad station.

Swinging into the driveway, Nancy Drew halted the roadster and sprang out, but before she could reach the house her father, suitcase in hand, came out the front door, followed by Hannah Gruen. The housekeeper was the first to catch sight of Nancy.

"Oh, Miss Nancy," she began apologetically, "I'm dreadfully sorry to leave you in a mess like this; but my poor sister——"

"Of course you must go," Nancy told her quickly. "Don't worry about me. I'll get along somehow."

"You're so kind, Miss Nancy. I'll come

back just the first minute I can, but it may be several months.''

''Stay as long as your sister needs you.''

''We must hurry if you're to catch your train, Hannah,'' Carson Drew interrupted. ''It's a long way to the station.''

He rushed the housekeeper to the waiting automobile and started the motor.

''Better get in touch with an employment agency right away,'' he called back to Nancy as the car moved away. Nancy watched the automobile until it was out of sight and then walked slowly toward the house. She knew that Hannah had indeed left her in a ''mess.''

Since the death of her mother many years before, Nancy Drew had managed the household. On the whole she had engineered everything so skillfully that her father little dreamed of the heavy responsibility which rested upon her shoulders.

As a famous criminal and mystery-case lawyer, Carson Drew found it necessary to maintain a certain social position, and accordingly Nancy was frequently called upon to entertain noted professional men.

She had often been present when Carson Drew discussed important cases with detectives and police officials, and as a result had become interested in detective work herself. Her first fame came when she uncovered "The Secret of the Old Clock."

Later she solved the mystery of a troubled household, discovering a hidden staircase and having no end of creepy adventures in an underground passageway.

Undaunted by this experience, she risked her life to help Laura Pendleton. Nancy's unusual adventures in this connection are recounted in the third volume of the series, "The Bungalow Mystery."

Now, as Nancy Drew walked slowly toward the house, she was considering the problem which Hannah Gruen's departure had created. Her father confidently expected that by the time Judge Graham arrived for his week-end visit the household would be moving as smoothly as before, but Nancy, who had tried many servants before she had secured Hannah, was beset with doubt.

"I'll telephone the agency right away and see what they can do for me," she decided.

Having looked up a number in the directory, she repeated it to an operator and after a brief wait was connected with the manager of the best employment agency in River Heights. She stated her wants briefly, trying not to appear too exacting.

"We'll do the best we can for you, Miss,"

came the not too comforting response. "But right now we have only one servant on hand—a colored woman."

"Send her out this afternoon," Nancy ordered in despair. "I must have someone immediately."

Replacing the telephone on the stand, she went to the kitchen to take stock of affairs there. As she had feared, everything was in confusion. In her haste Hannah had not even ordered the groceries for the following day.

Nancy set about putting things in order. While she was making out the grocery list, she heard her father's car on the drive.

"Well, did you get a maid?" he questioned a few minutes later when he entered the living room.

"Yes, the agency is sending out a colored woman this afternoon."

Nancy, observing that her father looked tired, refrained from adding that she feared the worst.

"I'm mighty glad you found someone," Carson Drew responded in relief. "You're a wonderful little manager. By the way, I suppose you delivered those papers to Judge Howell all right."

"Yes, I found him at the court house and had no trouble. On the way back I stopped at Lilac Inn for luncheon and ran into Emily

Crandall. She's celebrating her eighteenth birthday this week. According to her grandmother's will, she's to inherit the famous Crandall diamonds.''

Carson Drew whistled softly.

"Quite a windfall, I must say. I remember the Crandall jewels very well. They were very quaint and beautiful.''

"I'm so glad they were willed to Emily. She's never had many pretty things, especially since the death of her mother.''

"I hope she'll manage to hang on to them after they fall into her hands,'' Mr. Drew commented.

"Oh, I'm sure Emily won't let them slip through her fingers. She's not in the least extravagant.''

"I wasn't thinking of that. It merely occurred to me that unscrupulous persons may be interested in those jewels.''

Nancy nodded thoughtfully.

"I believe she intends to place them in a bank vault immediately.''

"A very wise precaution." Carson Drew lowered his voice as he heard a heavy step on the porch. Nancy sprang up from the davenport where she was sitting and rushed to the door.

"It must be the new housekeeper,'' she cried hopefully.

As she opened the door her heart sank within her. It was indeed the colored woman sent by the employment agency, but a more unlikely housekeeper Nancy had never seen. She was dirty and slovely in appearance and had an unpleasant way of shuffling her feet when she walked.

Inviting her into the house, Nancy asked a few questions which the woman answered in unsatisfactory manner. She was unable to produce references of any description.

"I'm very sorry, but I'm afraid you won't do," Nancy told her at last.

It was with a feeling of mingled disappointment and relief that she watched the woman depart. As a housekeeper, the Negress was impossible, and yet she wondered if she had been unwise to let her go. She must find someone!

Rushing to the telephone she called a number and was quickly connected with another employment agency. After a long discussion with the manager she finally secured a promise that a woman would be sent out early the next morning.

"I certainly hope she'll be better than the colored woman," Nancy sighed to her father. "I don't know why, but I have a feeling this servant problem will prove my undoing."

CHAPTER III

A Queer Girl

"Oh, Dad, you don't know what a time I've had!" Nancy Drew emitted a tired sigh as she emerged from the kitchen unfastening her apron. "This morning the agency sent me an Irish woman, but she was even worse than the one that came yesterday. She was the most unreasonable housekeeper I ever interviewed."

"Poor little girl," Mr. Drew sympathized. "I can't let you do the work yourself."

"Well, I think it will be easier on me than to try to break in a new girl. After the Irish woman left I called another agency and they sent me a Scotch lassie. She looked promising, but I found she hadn't had a particle of experience and knew little about cooking. I'm completely discouraged."

"I don't wonder, and with Judge Graham coming Saturday night."

"I'll find someone before that time if I have to coax her away from my best friend," Nancy declared resolutely. "There's one more agency that I haven't tried."

As soon as her father had finished luncheon and had left for his office, Nancy Drew again went to the telephone and was gratified when the employment agency promised to send out a girl at once. She was washing dishes when she heard a sharp knock on the front door. Drying her hands, she rusned into the hall to answer the summons.

As she swung open the massive oak door she beheld a tall, wiry, dark-complexioned girl who obviously was the one sent out from the agency. She had dark piercing eyes and stared at Nancy almost impudently.

Nancy resisted an impulse to shut the door in her face. She did not like the girl's sly look. On the other hand, she thought that it might not be fair to judge by appearances alone. Accordingly, she smiled pleasantly and invited the girl into the living room.

The stranger seated herself on the davenport, and to Nancy's amazement proceeded to look the house over most critically, darting quick little glances from one room to another.

"She's prying," Nancy thought. Aloud she said: "What is your name?"

"Mary Mason."

"Can you furnish references?"

The girl made no response, but from a dirty pocketbook brought out an envelope and handed it to Nancy. The envelope contained several references and Nancy glanced quickly over them. To her surprise, the girl came highly recommended from her former employers, and it appeared that she had held responsible positions. Nancy had been on the verge of dismissing the girl, but in the face of such excellent references she hesitated. She was not favorably impressed with Mary Mason, for the girl had a harsh face and a bold manner, but she knew that in all probability it would be impossible to find another girl before Saturday. She was left no choice in the matter.

"You appear quite young to take complete charge of the household," Nancy began doubtfully. "Do you feel sure you could manage the work? Of course I will direct you until you learn the routine."

Mary Mason tossed her head contemptuously.

"I always work without direction."

"Indeed?"

Nancy was still more unfavorably impressed and decided to ask the girl a few personal questions.

"Where is your home?"

"My home?" the girl looked startled, and then said quickly: "I haven't any real home. I'm an orphan."

"Oh," Nancy murmured, but for some reason which she could not understand she found it impossible to feel especially sympathetic. It even occurred to her that Mary Mason had deliberately told a falsehood, but she tried to force this suspicion from her mind. Probably it was only the girl's queer manner. "Your age?" she inquired.

"Eighteen."

Again Nancy was surprised, for she had made up her mind that Mary Mason was at least two years older than that. She next asked a few questions concerning the work which the girl had done in the past and was better pleased with her answers. It was evident that she could at least cook and keep house. Nancy decided that she would put up with her until after Judge Graham's visit. Perhaps she would adapt herself after she had been in the Drew household for a number of days.

"I will try you for a week," Nancy told her. "When can you come?"

"This afternoon if you want me. What salary can I expect?"

"Oh, yes, I forgot to mention that. I pay very well indeed, but in return I expect faithful service. I will start you at fifteen dollars a week with room and board. And of course you may have one day a week off."

Nancy Drew had expected that Mary Mason would express satisfaction at this arrangement, for the pay was much higher than the average in River Heights. Instead, the girl scowled darkly.

"Surely that is enough," Nancy said a trifle impatiently.

"Oh, I suppose it'll have to do; but it's not as much as I should have."

"I noticed in your references that you had been receiving only twelve dollars a week."

Mary Mason looked confused as though she had been trapped.

"Well, fifteen will do I guess."

"Then, if you are satisfied with the wage I will tell you something of the work. I am sure you will not find it particularly difficult; but as I stated, I am rather exacting about details. You see, because of my father's position it is necessary for us to do a great deal of entertaining."

"I'll have no trouble," the girl returned indifferently.

"Then I guess there is nothing more I need tell you until later. I will have your room ready for you when you return this afternoon with your things."

Mary Mason arose to depart. She sauntered across the floor, casting a last appraising glance about the room. Nancy escorted her to the door and as she opened it recalled that she had neglected to mention her own name.

"I am Nancy Drew," she said pleasantly.

Mary Mason's indifferent attitude vanished as if by magic.

"Nancy Drew?" she repeated tensely.

"Why, yes. You've heard of me perhaps?"

The girl ignored the question; in fact, she seemed not to have heard it. As Nancy stared at her in surprise she saw that the color had drained from her face, leaving it white and frightened.

"Who are you?" the girl demanded harshly. "You aren't the daughter of——"

"Carson Drew," Nancy finished. "You've probably heard of him."

"Your father is a lawyer?"

"Yes. He specializes in criminal and mystery cases."

The announcement had a very peculiar effect upon Mary Mason. She took a step backward and her hand gripped the door knob. Her eyes dilated with something that looked like fear.

"I can't take the position, Miss Drew," she said a trifle shakily.

"You can't take it? Why not, may I ask?"

"I—I didn't know your father was a lawyer."

"What difference can that make?" Nancy asked bluntly.

"I'll not work in such a place! I wouldn't think of it!"

"My father will be very kind to you. You

need have no fear on that score. I don't see why you should be afraid."

"Oh, I'm not afraid," Mary returned hastily. "It's just that I might get into trouble working at a place where the man of the house is always mixed up in queer cases. You'll have to find another girl."

"But it's so late, and I've had such a time! Judge Graham is coming this week and——"

"I tell you I won't stay," the girl broke in, becoming more excited.

"Even if I offer you eighteen instead of fifteen dollars a week? That's an outrageous amount!"

"I won't stay here under any condition. Let me out!"

Nancy Drew reluctantly stepped aside, and Mary Mason rushed out the door, fairly running across the porch in her haste to reach the street. Nancy, a puzzled expression on her face, stood in the doorway and watched her until she had rounded a corner.

"Can you beat that!" she exclaimed, lapsing into slang. "If she isn't the queerest girl I ever met! And to think I've wasted nearly an hour in talking to her!"

CHAPTER IV

About the Crandall Jewels

A LESS enterprising and resourceful girl than Nancy Drew would have been hopelessly discouraged at the turn events had taken. In truth, after Mary Mason's strange leave-taking Nancy was discouraged, but not hopelessly so. Deciding to transact no more business by telephone, she climbed into her roadster and set out to make the rounds of the employment agencies. The afternoon brought nothing but disappointment. She returned home tired but undaunted, and the following morning started out early, determined to make one last effort before admitting defeat.

It was not until late that day that fortune favored her. After interviewing no less than six girls who were utterly unfitted for the place, she chanced upon Mrs. Sadie Carter, an elderly woman who suited her in every way. Mrs. Carter was neat in appearance and thoroughly experienced. Her references were of the best and her demands not at all unrea-

sonable. Nancy was delighted and promptly
engaged her.

It took less than one day in the Drew household for Mrs. Carter to prove her worth.

"Don't you worry about a blessed thing,
Miss Nancy," the woman said to her. "I'll
tend to everything."

Nancy, satisfied that the new housekeeper
was dependable, was delighted to be relieved
of responsibility, especially as she was eager
to call upon Emily Crandall. She had not forgotten that she had been promised a glimpse of
the famous Crandall jewels and she had no intention of allowing the opportunity to slip
away.

Accordingly, after an early luncheon she
backed her roadster from the garage and set
off for the Crandall cottage on the lake. It was
with high anticipation that she walked up the
path to the house. She rapped on the door,
but there was no response. After a little wait,
she rapped again, louder than before. Still no
one came to open the door. Somewhat mysti-
fied, Nancy walked around the house. There
appeared to be no one at home.

"It's only ten minutes after one," Nancy
thought, glancing at her wrist watch. "Emily
probably didn't expect me this early. She
may come back later, but I don't believe I had

better wait. I can see the jewels at some later time.''

She returned to the roadster and after a moment's hesitation started the motor and headed for River Heights again. She had driven less than two miles when she noted the approach of a sedan.

"Why, I believe that's Mrs. Willoughby's sedan,'' she told herself. "It must be Emily.''

She brought the roadster to a halt and waved her hand. Instantly, there was a grinding of brakes and the sedan came to a stop alongside. Emily Crandall sprang from the car and came running over to the roadster.

"Oh, Nancy, I'm so sorry! I know you must have stopped at the cottage. I intended to get back before you came.''

"I just wanted to congratulate you on your birthday, Emily.''

"Thanks, Nancy. I'm as happy as a lark to-day.''

"Then you must have received your inheritance.''

Emily Crandall's pretty face clouded.

"The jewels haven't been turned over to me yet. I shan't get them until to-night.''

"How is that?''

"Well, you see they've been kept in a safety deposit box in another town. Mrs. Willoughby had to go after them to-day.''

"I should have thought you would have gone with her. I know I couldn't have waited."

"I did want to go, but Mrs. Willoughby went with a friend of hers—a Mrs. Potter. I'm not very crazy about her, and, anyway, there wasn't room in her coupé. I'll see the jewels to-night."

"Then you'll have to keep them in the cottage all night!"

"I suppose so."

"But aren't you afraid, Emily?"

"Yes, it does make me a trifle uneasy. But I guess they'll be safe enough. No one knows I'm inheriting them except you and Mrs. Potter."

"Oh, they'll probably be safe enough for one night," Nancy returned, for she did not wish to alarm Emily; "but it seems a shame they couldn't have been left in the safety deposit vault. Then there couldn't be any risk."

"That would have been wiser, I suppose," Emily said thoughtfully. "I wish now I'd told Mrs. Willoughby to leave them in the bank vault, but I've been perfectly crazy to see them."

"Can't you telephone her?"

"I'm afraid it's too late. She'll be on her way home by this time."

"You'll probably get your jewels all right," Nancy observed. "But it does seem to me that

Mrs. Willoughby is a trifle careless in removing them from the vault.''

"I guess that's just her way, Nancy. She always has been careless with things. Oh, dear, I wish I had gone with her!''

"I'm sorry I said anything, Emily. I didn't mean to disturb you.''

"Oh, I won't worry,'' Emily laughed. "I'm far too happy. Besides, we haven't had a robbery in or anywhere near River Heights for years.''

"I think you're a very lucky girl to be coming into such an inheritance,'' Nancy said easily.

"I am lucky!'' Emily's eyes began to dance and the troubled frown instantly melted from her forehead. "And just look at this!''

Proudly she displayed a glittering diamond on the third finger of her left hand.

"Emily Crandall! You're engaged!''

Emily nodded happily.

"I'll tell you all about it if you promise you won't repeat it to any of the girls.''

"Cross my heart.''

"I'm engaged to Dick Farnham. You've met him, Nancy. Don't you remember? He works at the Granger Manufacturing company.''

"Oh, yes, I remember! I wish you all kinds of happiness.''

"Dick and I would like to get married next

fall," Emily went on. "But right now he isn't making enough for us to live on."

"If I remember correctly, Dick has excellent chances," Nancy said politely.

"Oh, yes, he's certain to work into a better position in a few years. But it's so dreadfully hard to wait. He has a chance to buy out an established business for three thousand dollars, too. If he could only get started for himself, he'd soon make enough so we could get married."

"Hasn't he any savings?"

"Oh, yes! But not enough, and this deal requires cash. The worst of it is that he must raise it within the next few weeks or miss the opportunity."

"What a shame!"

"That's what I think. And I'll tell you what I intend to do, Nancy. You won't tell?"

"Of course not."

"I'm going to sell a few of those jewels and set Dick up in business. I know he will make good. Of course I intend to keep some of the jewels and maybe have them reset; but there's no use in keeping them all. They'd just lie around in a bank vault. Do you think I'm doing wrong to help Dick?"

"No, I don't," Nancy returned firmly. "I think it's very generous of you. I certainly wish you all joy."

"I felt sure you'd agree with me," Emily said eagerly. "And now since I've told you all my history, won't you come back with me to the cottage?"

"I really haven't time now, Emily; but I'll drive back to-morrow if I may."

"Fine! Then you'll get to see the jewels after all. I'll be looking for you."

With a wave of her hand, Emily Crandall returned to the sedan and drove away.

For several minutes Nancy Drew sat motionless in her roadster, staring fixedly straight before her.

"Emily would be broken-hearted if anything happened to those jewels," she thought. Then she shrugged her shoulders and shifted gears. "What's the matter with me, anyway? Always borrowing trouble!"

CHAPTER V

AT LILAC INN

As NANCY DREW drove slowly back toward River Heights she tried to persuade herself that her fears concerning the Crandall jewels were groundless. She did not fully succeed in doing this.

In fact, at the very moment she said good-bye to Emily Crandall, startling events were taking place only a few miles away. Had Nancy Drew been at Lilac Inn she would have seen a handsome coupé swing up to the door from which two elegantly dressed women alighted. Nancy would have recognized Mrs. Jane Willoughby and her friend, Mrs. Clara Potter.

As the two women stepped from the car Mrs. Willoughby cast a quick glance about and nervously clutched a handbag which she carried. Mrs. Potter kept close at her side.

"Do you think it was wise to stop here for luncheon?" Mrs. Potter asked in a low tone. "We can't take any chances, carrying all that precious jewelry."

"Hush!" her companion commanded sharply. "No one must know I have it!"

The two women walked swiftly up the path to Lilac Inn and entered the dining room. As the hour was early the room was but half filled and the ladies were led at once to a table by a window. As the two seated themselves, many of the diners turned to stare curiously, for it was obvious from the nervous manner in which Mrs. Willoughby clutched her handbag, that she was carrying something valuable. Mrs. Willoughby, innocently unaware that she had given herself away, placed the handbag on the table and sighed in relief as she unfastened her wrap.

"I'm sure no one suspects that we are carrying valuables, Clara. However, I shall feel very much relieved when I have Emily's receipt for what I am carrying."

"Mercy, but it's warm in here—or perhaps it's the excitement. Don't you think we should have a window open?"

"By all means, Clara." Mrs. Willoughby motioned to a waiter. "We would like this window raised," she told him.

The waiter glanced curiously at the large handbag which rested upon the table, for the clasp was ornate, set rather lavishly with stones, and with a polite bow opened the window. He then took the order and departed

"Did you notice the way he looked at that purse?" Mrs. Willoughby whispered.

"Yes, I did. But he couldn't know what was in it, I'm sure."

"Just the same, I almost wish we hadn't stopped here. This place is beginning to give me the creeps."

"I know just how you feel, Jane. I have the same sensation myself—just as if someone were listening to our conversation."

Mrs. Willoughby laughed nervously.

"Aren't we silly, Clara? The other diners aren't paying a particle of attention to us."

"That woman over in the corner seems to be watching us, Jane. The one with the piercing black eyes. I don't like her looks."

Mrs. Willoughby glanced quickly toward the woman indicated and nodded in agreement.

"She does seem to be especially interested in what we are doing, doesn't she? But of course she can't know that we are carrying valuables. We haven't told a soul."

"I suppose we're just nervous. Of course she can't know that the jewels are in the handbag. After all, the bag is a beauty and well worth looking at, and it is oversize for ordinary use. Well, here comes the waiter with our luncheon. We can eat quickly and get away."

As the waiter placed the steaming dishes

upon the table, Mrs. Willoughby watched him closely. She decided that she did not like the way he kept looking at her handbag. Finally, he brought the salad, and before Mrs. Willoughby could stop him he lifted the purse to make room for the plates.

"Don't touch that!" she said sharply.

Mrs. Willoughby had not intended that her voice should carry, but to her embarrassment several diners glanced at her curiously.

"I beg your pardon, madam," the waiter said politely, giving her a quick look.

"Oh, I see," Mrs. Willoughby murmured apologetically as she saw that the waiter had merely intended to move the purse to a more convenient place on the table. "That's all right."

The waiter returned to the kitchen with his tray and Mrs. Willoughby and her friend exchanged anxious glances.

"He must have felt how heavy it was when he lifted it, Clara!"

"Yes. But I feel sure the help at Lilac Inn is reliable," Mrs. Potter said comfortingly. "The management would have to be careful, you know, in order to maintain the excellent reputation of the place."

"Probably you are right. But I shall keep my eye on that handbag every minute."

"Yes, it doesn't pay to be careless."

Conversation lagged as the two women turned their attention to luncheon. They were both eager to get away from Lilac Inn, though neither was willing to admit her growing nervousness. At last, to their relief, the waiter appeared with dessert and coffee.

Mrs. Willoughby had scarcely touched a spoon to her orange ice when a woman who was sitting on the opposite side of the room gave a little scream of fright.

Instantly every eye turned her way. Mrs. Willoughby's spoon clattered against the plate. Mrs. Potter sprang to her feet and she too gave a cry of alarm.

"Look at those two automobiles!"

"Someone is going to be killed!"

It was all over in an instant. To the horror-stricken diners there came the sound of a terrific crash. Two automobiles had collided at the crossroads.

Chairs were hastily pushed back and everyone rushed to the doors and windows. For several minutes everything was in confusion. In her haste to see what had happened, Mrs. Willoughby upset a glass of water. Even the waiters dropped their trays and ran to the door.

"I saw it all!" Mrs. Potter cried. "I'm sure someone must have been killed! The cars came together with terrific force!"

"Oh, how dreadful!" Mrs. Willoughby moaned. "Why will people insist upon speeding?"

"Send for a doctor and an ambulance!" Mrs. Potter cried.

Several men rushed from the dining room and hurried toward the scene of the accident. One of the waiters sprang to a telephone and quickly called the nearest doctor. The room was abuzz with excited conversation.

"It was their own fault," someone declared emphatically. "I saw it all from this window. Both cars were going at terrific speed."

"Oh, I hope no one was killed," Mrs. Willoughby murmured anxiously.

For a few minutes it seemed that everyone talked at once, relating what each had witnessed. The commotion died down as the manager of the tea room, an elderly, pleasant-faced woman, came up the path.

"It's all right," she informed the diners. "Fortunately, no one was seriously injured. Both cars were completely wrecked."

"What a relief," Mrs. Willoughby sighed, as she turned away from the window.

Nearly all of the diners went back to their tables and Mrs. Willoughby and her companion among them. As Mrs. Potter sank down into her chair, her eyes swept the table in amazement.

"Oh, Jane!" she cried in alarm. "Your bag! You picked it up, didn't you?"

Mrs. Willoughby rushed to the table, her face expressing genuine horror.

"No, I thought you did!"

"I didn't touch the bag. When I heard that terrible crash I forgot all about it."

"It must be here somewhere. Look under the table."

Mrs. Potter jerked up the table cloth, but there was no sign of the handbag on the floor.

"It isn't here, Jane."

With a low moan, Mrs. Willoughby sank into a chair.

"Oh, what shall I do?" she wailed. "Some-one has stolen it! Emily's inheritance!"

"I can't believe it!" cried Mrs. Potter fran-dically. "The purse must be here! But per-haps you dropped it in your chair," she sug-gested hopefully.

"No, I've looked there. And it isn't on the floor. Oh, what shall I do?"

"Are you sure it didn't drop behind the table? Here, let me pull it out."

Mrs. Potter grasped the edge of the table as she spoke and pulled it away from the win-dow. The missing handbag was not revealed!

CHAPTER VI

ACCUSATIONS

BY THIS time a number of the diners, attracted by the strange actions and excited voices of the two women, had crowded about them. The manager came hurrying up to inquire what the trouble was.

"My handbag!" Mrs. Willoughby wailed. "Someone has taken it!"

"Oh, there must be a mistake," the manager assured her.

"There's no mistake. I left it on the table when I ran to the window at the sound of the crash. I couldn't have had my back turned more than a minute. When I rushed back to the table my handbag was gone."

"This is very serious, Madam. Are you certain you did not have the bag in your hand when you left the table?"

Miserably, Mrs. Willoughby shook her head. "I'm sure I didn't."

"Someone must have stolen it," Mrs. Potter interposed. "That's the only explanation."

"I'll never leave this place until I get my

38

handbag back!" Mrs. Willoughby screamed hysterically. "I'll have everyone searched!"

"Just a minute, please," the cool voice of the manager interposed. "Let me get this straight. How much do you claim that you lost?"

"Claim?" Mrs. Willoughby cried angrily. "Do you mean to insinuate that my handbag wasn't stolen?"

"I am not insinuating anything. I am merely trying to get at the bottom of the matter. How much money did you have in your purse?"

"Not a cent in money, but I had a fortune in jewels! Forty thousand dollars' worth of jewels, mostly diamonds, and they didn't belong to me!"

There was a surprised chorus of "oh's" from those who had gathered about, and at once many of the diners began to search the floor and near-by tables. No trace of the handbag was found.

"I regret that such a thing has happened in my tea room," the manager said, with a troubled frown. "But of course it was very unwise of you to bring such an amount into the dining room. We provide a safe for our customers' valuables. Since you did not choose to make use of it, the management is in no way responsible for your loss. However, I will do everything in my power to help you recover the jewels.''

''They were stolen by someone in this room!'' Mrs. Willoughby cried excitedly. ''I insist that every person be searched.''

The manager hesitated, for she felt that such a procedure might arouse the ire of her customers, especially those who were socially prominent.

''I for one am willing to submit to a search,'' a feminine guest declared quickly.

Others expressed their willingness to subject themselves to the ordeal. Of all the guests, only two women insisted that the search would be an indignity. One of these, the dark woman who had attracted the attention of Mrs. Willoughby and Mrs. Potter some time before, tried to slip out of the door.

''Don't let her go!'' Mrs. Potter cried. ''She must be searched with the others!''

''I have nothing to conceal,'' the woman retorted with a show of hauteur.

''We will see about that,'' Mrs. Willoughby snapped.

''You'll see yourself if you persist in this indignity!'' exclaimed the woman, a spot of scarlet flaming into each cheek.

''Perhaps it will be best for you to submit to the search,'' the manager suggested in a conciliatory voice. ''If you ladies will step into the adjoining cloakroom one by one I will make the search myself.''

Again the black-eyed woman began to protest angrily, but her companion, who had been the only other person to object to the search, said a few words in an undertone and the enraged woman closed her mouth in a grim line and said no more.

While Mrs. Willoughby and her friend waited anxiously in the dining room, the search was conducted. Within fifteen minutes the clothing of every guest had been examined, including that of the woman who had attempted to escape from the inn. The manager shook her head regretfully as she returned to Mrs. Willoughby.

''I did not find the jewels.''

''Then some of the help must have taken it.''

''I can vouch for every person in my employ. I demand the highest references.''

''Well, someone took the pocketbook! It couldn't have walked off by itself! I saw one of the waiters looking at it and when he brought the salad——''

''Jennings has been in my employ for six years,'' the manager said quietly. ''But if it will rest your mind on that score, I am certain he will submit to a search.''

''Certainly.''

The waiter stepped forward, bestowing a not

too kindly glance upon the two women. One of the men in the room offered to conduct the search. In a very few minutes he returned, but without the pocketbook.

"The kitchen help must be brought in," Mrs. Willoughby insisted.

"Really this is going a trifle too far," the manager said impatiently. "As I told you, I can vouch for all my help. And of course the kitchen girls never enter this room. It is ridiculous to think that one of them could have taken your bag."

"Someone took it."

"Are you certain that you had the handbag when you came into the dining room?" This came in a drawling voice from one of the women who had been searched.

"Am I certain?" Mrs. Willoughby screamed as she sprang up from the chair into which she had dropped in exhaustion. "Of course I am!"

Until this moment Mrs. Willoughby had controlled herself fairly well, but the realization that people were beginning to doubt her own honesty entirely unnerved her. She began to pace the floor, wringing her hands.

"Oh, what shall I do? What shall I do? I'll never be able to face Emily."

"Try to calm yourself," the manager begged.

"I can't be calm! I've lost poor Emily's fortune! Oh, I wish I were dead!"

"Jane! Jane!" Mrs. Potter pleaded.

Mrs. Willoughby paid not the slightest heed to her friend but suddenly wheeled upon the staring guests.

"Is anyone missing who was here when the accident occurred?" she demanded.

A check-up was hastily made and it was found that two persons were missing.

"They're probably at the crossroads helping those poor autoists," the manager suggested.

Mrs. Willoughby, becoming more excited every moment, appeared not to have heard.

"One of them must have snatched my purse and run away with it!" she screamed. "Oh, help me catch the thief!"

She rushed toward the door, but before she reached it gave a low moan of pain and clutched at a table. She would have fallen to the floor had not Mrs. Potter caught her in her arms.

"It's her heart!" Mrs. Potter cried. "The excitement has been too much for her. Oh, she's fainted."

Willing hands aided Mrs. Potter in stretching the limp figure out upon a couch. Someone brought a pitcher of water. A damp cloth was pressed against Mrs. Willoughby's forehead and her hands were chafed. After a few minutes she began to revive.

"What will Emily say when I tell her?" she moaned over and over.

The bystanders murmured, some sympathetically, some skeptically.

"She will be all right in a few minutes," Mrs. Potter said. "She has had trouble with her heart before. Poor thing! I don't wonder that she fainted."

As soon as Mrs. Willoughby was able to sit up, the manager suggested that she be removed to another room.

"No, I feel better now," Mrs. Willoughby said weakly. "I can walk to the automobile."

In spite of the protests of those who had attended her, she insisted upon departing. Leaning heavily upon Mrs. Potter's arm, she moved slowly toward the door.

"I'm sure we'll find the handbag for you," the manager said kindly.

Mrs. Willoughby shook her head.

"I'm convinced someone snatched it and ran away. I'll probably never see the jewels again. Oh, my poor little Emily! How can I tell her?"

CHAPTER VII

DAMAGING RUMORS

"Ho-HUM, but I'm tired to-night. Hard day at the office."

Carson Drew dropped his hat on the living room table and sank wearily on the davenport. "By the way, Nancy, I suppose you've heard the bad news by this time."

"What news?" Nancy demanded anxiously. "Don't dare tell me that Judge Graham isn't coming after all the trouble I've had getting a satisfactory housekeeper."

"Oh, Judge Graham will get here all right. I was referring to the news about your little friend, Emily Crandall."

"Emily? Why, I saw her only this afternoon."

"But you didn't see the Crandall jewels."

"Why, no, her guardian was to deliver them later in the day."

"Read this!"

Mr. Drew spread out the front page of the evening paper before his daughter's startled eyes.

"The Crandall jewels—stolen!" Nancy gasped. "Oh, how dreadful!"

"I can't say that it surprises me much," Mr. Drew commented dryly. "Mrs. Willoughby didn't appear to have used an ounce of sense. She invited trouble by carrying forty thousand dollars' worth of diamonds unguarded."

"What a blow this will be to Emily, Dad. Why, she has counted on her inheritance for everything! Now, she won't be able to help Dick."

"It's a shame, all right," Mr. Drew agreed.

"Surely, she won't lose her entire inheritance, Father. The jewels were never turned over to her. Couldn't Mrs. Willoughby be held responsible?"

"That's a legal question, Nancy."

"But the loss was due to her carelessness."

"Apparently so. But the court would demand absolute proof. Emily would have to bring suit against her guardian."

"I suppose she'll never do that," Nancy said thoughtfully. "Emily told me that she is fond of her guardian."

"Moreover, it's very doubtful that she could collect a cent if she did bring suit. Even if she won the case I don't see that she would gain much."

"Why, I thought Mrs. Willoughby had a great deal of money."

"She did at one time. But I've been told that most of it has slipped through her fingers. Mrs. Willoughby has lived a bit high, Nancy. She likes to move in gay society and associate with expensive friends."

"Mrs. Potter for instance."

"Yes. While her husband was alive, Mrs. Willoughby never had to think about money matters. Unfortunately, she is not a good business woman."

"Are you certain she is in straitened circumstances?" Nancy inquired anxiously.

"I am sure of it. I was told that only last week she applied at the bank for a loan of five thousand dollars and was refused."

"What an unfortunate time for her to lose Emily's inheritance," Nancy said significantly.

"Yes, it's beginning to look bad for her. Rumors are circulating even now."

"What are people saying?"

"It's being hinted that Mrs. Willoughby had designs on Emily's fortune herself."

"But she was always so kind to Emily."

"I know. Mind, I'm telling you only what others are saying."

"What do you believe?"

"My dear child," and Mr. Drew smiled, "I wouldn't venture an opinion. I always reserve judgment until I have all of the facts."

Nancy glanced thoughtfully at the account in the paper.

"It says here that she fainted when she learned that the bag had been stolen. That looks as though she felt the loss most keenly."

"Unless she was acting."

"You don't think that the robbery was a frame-up, do you?" Nancy asked, in astonishment.

"You're a regular detective when it comes to pinning a fellow down," Mr. Drew complained good-naturedly. "I am merely considering the possibility. As I understand it, Mrs. Willoughby had access to the safety deposit box containing the jewels. It would not have been difficult for her to have pawned them weeks ago, perhaps substituting paste. Then the little scene at Lilac Inn could have been staged."

"But this account says that Mrs. Willoughby actually carried a handbag into the inn," Nancy reminded her father. "Several persons noticed it—it was conspicuous—and how uneasily she acted. There is no question that the purse mysteriously disappeared. What became of it?"

"That's what the police would like to know," Mr. Drew replied.

"Of course, if Mrs. Willoughby had been

staging the whole scene, it might have been possible for her to have secreted the purse somewhere.''

"Or Mrs. Potter may have taken it.''

"That's another angle to consider, all right. The paper says she wasn't searched.''

"It's a baffling mystery, Nancy. Perhaps you'd better take a hand in it.''

"Don't make fun of me, Dad.''

"I'm not. I have great respect for your ability in tracking down a mystery. In fact, once or twice you've rather shown your old dad up.''

"You know I haven't,'' Nancy protested, highly pleased. "But there's something about this mystery that catches my interest, and of course I'd give anything to help Emily Crandall regain her inheritance.''

"Unless I miss my guess, this Crandall affair will prove more baffling that any other case you ever attacked. You might try your teeth on it.''

Nancy Drew's eyes began to sparkle, but she shook her head.

"I wouldn't think of interfering—that is, unless Emily asked me to.''

"Perhaps it's just as well that you shouldn't get mixed up in it. This isn't an ordinary robbery.''

"Haven't the police any real clue?"

"They're inclined to suspect Mrs. Willoughby."

"The police have been known to blunder."

"Yes. But sometimes, too, they are right, and this time they may not be far off the track. At least Mrs. Willoughby will bear watching. I wouldn't enjoy being in her shoes."

"Nor would I. I met her a number of months ago, but I haven't a very vivid recollection of what she is like."

"A charming woman, in appearance at least. However, you can't tell to what lengths a person will go when in desperate need of money."

"Emily will be crushed if she learns that her guardian is suspected. I have a notion to run out to the cottage and see her."

"Why don't you? I imagine she's all broken up over the loss of the jewels."

Nancy glanced at her watch.

"It's getting late. Still, it won't be dark for at least an hour. I'll do it!"

Hurrying to her room, she snatched up her hat and came clattering down the stairs two at a time.

"Good-bye, Dad," she called, as she started toward the back door. "I won't be gone long."

Mr. Drew did not reply, for just at that moment there was a step on the veranda.

Nancy paused and glanced questioningly toward her father.

"I'll wait and see who it is," she decided. "It may be someone for me."

The doorbell rang sharply, but before Nancy could retrace her steps the housekeeper opened the door. There was a murmur of voices in the outside hall and then Mrs. Carter appeared with a small calling card which she handed to Mr. Drew.

"She says it's very important that she see you to-night," the housekeeper reported.

Mr. Drew glanced carelessly at the card, and then his eyebrows lifted slightly. He turned to Nancy with a peculiar expression.

"It's Mrs. Willoughby," he said quietly. "I wonder what she wants of me."

"Perhaps I'd better leave the room," Nancy suggested. "Mrs. Willoughby may wish to talk with you privately."

"Stay if you like and hear what she has to say," Mr. Drew responded. "You're as much interested in the case as I am."

He turned to the housekeeper who was awaiting his decision.

"Kindly ask Mrs. Willoughby to come in."

CHAPTER VIII

Mrs. Willoughby's Call

The housekeeper vanished at Mr. Drew's words to reappear almost at once followed by the elegant Mrs. Willoughby. Mr. Drew arose and politely offered her a chair. Mrs. Carter discreetly withdrew.

"Oh, Mr. Drew, I'm in such trouble!" The visitor stopped short as she noticed Nancy for the first time.

"Don't mind my daughter. Anything that you may say will be held in strict confidence. Nancy is a close friend of your ward's and will help you if she can."

"Then you've already heard?"

The lawyer indicated the evening paper.

"I read the account in the paper. Were the details correct?"

"In the main," Mrs. Willoughby admitted reluctantly. "Oh, it's dreadful! Emily is heartbroken!"

Nancy, who was studying the woman closely, tried to make up her mind whether or not she was pretending. Either she was an excellent actress or genuinely agitated.

"Mr. Drew, you must help me," Mrs. Willoughby went on. "I feel my position keenly. Even the police are blaming me. It's so unjust."

"Has your ward accused you?"

"Oh, no! Emily wouldn't think of doing that. She's been wonderful. But the loss of the jewels will leave her destitute. I can't bear to think that I am the cause of it all." Mrs. Willoughby began to sob into her handkerchief.

Mr. Drew glanced quickly at his daughter, and Nancy gave an emphatic nod of her head, as much as to say that she would like to probe more deeply into the case and wanted her father to help her.

"There, Mrs. Willoughby," he said kindly, "don't take on. I will do anything in my power to aid you."

"You will? Oh, I'm so relieved!" The woman ceased crying and actually smiled. "I know everything will be all right now."

"I am not certain that I can recover the jewels for you," Mr. Drew pointed out; "so you mustn't build up your hopes too soon. The case will be a very difficult one."

Mrs. Willoughby's face clouded again.

"I didn't ask about your fee," she stammered. "I am afraid I must tell you that I haven't a great deal of money at present."

"I assure you my fee will be very reasonable. And now perhaps you will answer a few questions concerning the robbery."

"Anything!"

"Have you any theory as to what became of the handbag?"

"Oh, yes! I'm sure it was snatched by one of the inn guests at the time of that frightful automobile accident. When we checked up later, two of the guests were missing."

"Are you certain they had not gone to help at the scene of the wreck?"

"Well, at the time of the crash, a number of persons ran out of the inn. After the victims had been rushed to the hospital, all came back except these two."

"Do you know who they were?"

"No. Mrs. Potter and I hurried to the crossroads just as soon as I was able to walk—I fainted, you know. There wasn't a sign of anyone near the wreck."

"Perhaps the two who left the inn took the victims to the hospital," Mr. Drew suggested.

"That's so. I hadn't thought of that."

"In that event, their hasty leave-taking would be perfectly natural. Of course, one of the persons might have snatched your purse and used the accident as a pretext to get away."

"That's what I thought," Mrs. Willoughby said eagerly.

"The clue will bear investigation," Mr. Drew continued; "but I am inclined to believe it will not lead to anything."

"After all, it may have been the waiter. I was suspicious of him from the moment I stepped into the inn. He kept looking at my handbag."

"I understand he submitted to a search."

"Yes, I insisted upon it. The jewels weren't found upon his person, but he might have hidden them."

"I see by the paper that the handbag was rather larger than those usually carried and was highly ornamented."

"Yes. I knew I should need a large bag for those jewels. Still, it was not so large that it could not be stolen and concealed."

"Do you recall whether the waiter left the dining room during the confusion?"

"I really can't say," Mrs. Willoughby confessed. "I was so terribly excited myself."

"Could this waiter have known that you were carrying valuables in your purse?"

"He might have heard Mrs. Potter and me talking about it."

"You were speaking loudly?"

"Oh, no! We scarcely raised our voices above a whisper."

"I see." Mr. Drew thoughtfully tapped a pencil against the arm of his chair. After a moment he studied Mrs. Willoughby again.

"Tell me, were all of the guests searched?"

"Yes. Two women protested but finally gave in."

"How about Mrs. Potter?"

"Mrs. Potter? I don't understand."

"Was your friend searched with the others?"

"Certainly not," Mrs. Willoughby returned a trifle tartly. "It would have been insulting for me to have requested it."

"You feel then that she is trustworthy."

"Absolutely."

"How long have you known her?"

"Oh, a year at least."

"Hm," the lawyer mused. "Mrs. Willoughby, when you ran to the window, what did Mrs. Potter do?"

"What did she do?" Mrs. Willoughby asked a trifle impatiently. "Why, I don't remember exactly. She screamed and rushed to the window too, I believe."

"Then she was beside you every moment."

"N-o," Mrs. Willoughby admitted slowly. "We weren't at the same window. Really, I can't see the sense of these questions. Mrs. Potter had nothing to do with the loss of the handbag."

"Probably not," Mr. Drew agreed soothingly. "But I am trying to get at the bottom of the affair, and to do that I must investigate every clue."

"Mrs. Potter is my best friend. She would have no reason for stealing the jewels."

Seeing that Mrs. Willoughby was becoming agitated again, Mr. Drew decided to terminate the interview.

"I believe I have nothing more to ask you," he told her.

"You'll get the jewels back for me?"

"My dear Mrs. Willoughby, I can't make rash promises. As I told you before, the case is complicated. I will do my best to help you, though at the present time I am busy with other work. It seems to me that it might be wise for you to turn the affair over to a detective."

Mrs. Willoughby shook her head as she arose to leave.

"No, I've heard a great deal about your work, Mr. Drew, and I want you to take the case."

"Very well, I will report to you as soon as I learn anything of importance. In the meantime, do not discuss the case with anyone."

The lawyer escorted Mrs. Willoughby to the door and waited until she had left the porch before turning to Nancy.

"Well, little Golden Locks, what do you think of her?"

"Quite frivolous, but apparently honest," Nancy returned slowly. "It's a real mystery, isn't it? Do you really suspect Mrs. Willoughby?"

"No, or I shouldn't have taken the case even for your sake and for Emily's. Still, she is far from being free from suspicion. Any one of a number of persons might have stolen the jewels."

"I'd like to meet Mrs. Potter and hear her version of the robbery," said Nancy slowly.

"Yes, I must ask her to come to my office tomorrow." Mr. Drew frowned. "Hang it all, I have an important conference! I really haven't time for this case."

"I wish I could take it," Nancy murmured wistfully.

Mr. Drew studied his daughter meditatively.

"Well, why not?"

"I'm afraid it's too complicated for me. Anyway, Emily might feel that I was interfering."

"If you're still planning on running out to see her, you'd better hurry. It's getting late."

"I'll go now."

Nancy caught up her hat and with a hurried good-bye dashed out the back door to the garage. In a few minutes she was speeding toward the cottage on the lake.

"I hope Mrs. Willoughby doesn't get there before I do," she thought. "I'd rather talk to Emily alone."

After a short drive she came within sight of the cottage and was relieved to see that a light was shining through the windows. Parking the roadster, she hurried up the path and rapped on the door.

"Nancy!" Emily gasped, as she flung open the door to admit her friend. "Oh, I'm so glad you came!"

"You've been crying," Nancy observed quietly.

"I've lost my inheritance, Nancy. Mrs. Willoughby thinks we'll get the jewels back, but I'm sure we'll not. I was counting on the money so much! Now I can't help Dick!"

As Emily Crandall spoke she looked away and tried to keep back the tears. She did not succeed, and when the two girls entered the living room she flung herself on the couch and burst into a paroxysm of weeping.

"Oh, it's too dreadful, Nancy," she sobbed. "To have this inheritance come to me and then have it snatched away just when I'd planned to do so much with it! It's the loss of my grandmother's jewels and my not being able to help Dick and having to postpone my marriage, all jumbled into one!"

Nancy waited for a few minutes, then as the sobs grew quieter said comfortingly:

"Perhaps the fortune will be recovered."

"I'm afraid not. It seems to me the police are just going around in circles. By this time the thief is probably safe in another state."

"It's too mean for anything," Nancy went on. "I wish there was something I could do."

Emily glanced up quickly as a thought occurred to her.

"Why can't you help me?" she demanded tensely. "You've helped lots of other people!"

"I don't want to interfere. The police——"

"Oh, the police!" Emily dismissed them with a wave of her hand. "You're a wonder when it comes to solving a mystery! Will you help me?"

Nancy Drew hesitated and then nodded.

"I'll do my best."

"Oh, fine!" Emily's relief was evident. "The jewels are as good as found this minute!"

Nancy Drew smiled at her friend's returning good spirits, but as she walked down the path a few minutes later the smile faded from her face. She was eager to help Emily and pleased at an opportunity to "try her teeth" on a baffling mystery, but well she knew that she faced the most difficult task of her career.

CHAPTER IX

NANCY INVESTIGATES

"SINCE I talked with Mrs. Willoughby last evening, I've decided that I can't take her case after all."

Carson Drew pushed back his empty coffee cup as he addressed his daughter who sat opposite him at the breakfast table.

"You can't take it? Why not?"

"I forgot all about a case I have coming up this week. I'll be in court and shan't have time to think of anything else. I must ask Mrs. Willoughby to turn the matter over to another lawyer."

Nancy frowned, for this did not suit her plans at all.

"Why not turn it over to me, Dad?"

"But you said you didn't want to get mixed up in it."

"I've changed my mind. I talked with Emily Crandall last night and she wants me to help her if I can."

"Do you feel that you can handle the affair? It has the earmarks of a baffling mystery."

"I like them baffling," and Nancy grinned. "If I don't have any luck you can turn the case over to another lawyer."

"All right, go ahead. Have you any clue?"

"Not a one," Nancy admitted. "I thought I would drive over and interview Mrs. Potter. Then I intend to motor to Lilac Inn and talk with the manager."

"An excellent start. I wish you luck."

"I'll probably need it."

Ten o'clock found Nancy Drew driving toward the home of Mrs. Clara Potter. A trifle uncertainly, for she did not know what sort of reception to expect, she drew up in front of a large white house and walked toward the veranda. She noticed that the grounds were well kept and saw a gardener working in the flower beds.

"Mrs. Potter doesn't appear to be poverty-stricken, at least," Nancy told herself.

She lifted the door knocker, and presently was admitted by a trim maid. Nancy explained that she wished to see Mrs. Potter, and after a short wait was admitted to the lady's boudoir. Mrs. Potter, languid in an exquisite lounging robe, was just finishing her breakfast, but she arose at once to greet her caller. Nancy introduced herself, explaining her mission.

"Certainly, I'll tell you all I know about the robbery," Mrs. Potter declared, offering Nancy a seat. "I feel very sorry for poor Jane, but I must say she brought disaster upon herself. I warned her that it was unwise to carry those jewels the way she did."

Mrs. Potter then gave her account of the robbery, which tallied with the story Mrs. Willoughby had already given out.

"Did you see Mrs. Willoughby place the handbag on the table?" Nancy questioned, when Mrs. Potter had finished her tale.

"Yes, I did."

"Did you know that it contained the Crandall jewels?"

Mrs. Potter hesitated.

"Well, I didn't actually see the jewels. I went with Jane to the bank, but I remained in an outside room while she entered the vault."

"I see. Have you any reason to believe that Mrs. Willoughby might not have taken the jewels from the vault?"

"Certainly not."

"I have been told that Mrs. Willoughby is in rather straitened circumstance," Nancy said, hoping to draw Mrs. Potter out.

"Yes, Jane has been having trouble with her finances," the other admitted. "A few weeks ago I offered to lend her five hundred dollars."

"She accepted?"

"Yes. But a few days later she came to me and said that she did not require the money."

Nancy felt that this information was valuable, and quickly asked another question.

"Do you know where she secured the money which she evidently needed?"

"I didn't feel that it was my concern." Mrs. Potter looked troubled. "I hope you don't think that poor Jane planned that robbery herself."

"I am merely tracing down a number of clues," Nancy replied simply. "I understand that you were the first to discover that the handbag was missing."

"Yes," Mrs. Potter agreed noncommittally, her expression hardening.

"Have you any theory as to what became of it?"

"No."

It was evident to Nancy that Mrs. Potter was no longer willing to answer her questions; so after a little she said good-bye and left the house.

"I wonder if she was trying to hide something," Nancy Drew mused as she drove toward Lilac Inn. "She certainly closed up quickly enough when I started to question her about her own actions."

She was still considering Mrs. Potter's apparent unwillingness to answer personal questions when she reached Lilac Inn. As it was early in the morning she found the place deserted of guests and had no difficulty in finding the manager.

"Certainly, I'll be very glad to answer any of your questions," the woman agreed readily after Nancy had explained who she was. "Step into my office where we shall be undisturbed."

"Thank you," Nancy returned pleasantly. "But if you don't mind, I would like to see the table where Mrs. Willoughby sat."

"Why, of course. Right this way. She sat at this table by the window."

Nancy glanced at the table and then stepped to the window and looked out upon the rear veranda.

"As I understand it, Mrs. Willoughby ran to the window on the opposite side of the room when the crash came," the manager explained. "From where she sat it was impossible to see the crossroads."

"And during the brief time that her back was turned the handbag disappeared?"

"So Mrs. Willoughby claims."

"Do you doubt her story then?" Nancy demanded quickly.

"I really can't say," the manager evaded. "After the accident took place, I rushed outside with a number of the others. When I returned I learned that the purse had disappeared."

"I have been told that two of the guests failed to return to the dining room after the accident."

"I took it upon myself to investigate that angle, Miss Drew. I called the Mercy Hospital this morning and learned that the victims of the automobile accident were brought there by two persons who had been dining here."

"Then you discredit Mrs. Willoughby's theory that her purse was snatched by one of the guests."

"Yes, I do."

Nancy Drew accepted this for what it was worth, making ample allowance for the fact that the manager undoubtedly was bent on preserving the reputation of Lilac Inn. She determined that she would not drop this clue without a little investigation of her own.

"How about your help?" she inquired, starting out on a new line. "Are you sure that everyone in your employ is honest?"

"Yes. I am very particular. The handbag could not have been taken by anyone who works at the Inn."

"How many waiters were in the dining room at the time when Mrs. Willoughby discovered her loss?"

"I employ fifteen waiters. Eight or nine were in the room, I should judge."

"Were they all searched?"

"No, only Jennings. He served Mrs. Willoughby."

"Why were the others not searched?"

"I did not deem it necessary. They were occupied at tables in other parts of the room and could not have snatched the purse without being detected."

"May I talk with Jennings, please?"

"Certainly. But it will only be a waste of time. He had nothing to do with the robbery, I am sure."

"If you please, I think I will ask him a few questions."

"I'll call him."

The manager stepped to the kitchen door. Presently she returned, followed by Jennings. He was tall, precise in gait, and a trifle sullen in appearance. He regarded Nancy Drew with obvious misgiving.

"Jennings," the girl began quietly, "where were you at the time of the automobile accident?"

"I was on my way to the kitchen with a tray of dishes, Miss. Someone let out a scream. I set the tray on a table and ran to the door to see what had happened."

"On your way to the door did you pass Mrs. Willoughby's table?"

"No, Miss."

"At any time did you notice Mrs. Willough-by's purse?"

The waiter hesitated before answering this question and Nancy regarded him sharply.

"I saw it when I was serving her."

"And at the time of the alarm?"

"I did not look that way."

"Well, I believe that will be all. No, I have one more question. What do you think became of the handbag?"

"I couldn't rightly say, Miss. I only know that I didn't like the looks of that woman with Mrs. Willoughby. She was a queer one."

"Queer? In what way?"

The waiter shrugged his shoulders.

"I can't rightly say—it was just a feeling I had. Now if you've finished with me I'll go back to my work."

Nancy nodded absently and the waiter departed with alacrity.

"Do you wish to question any of the others?" the manager asked politely.

"Perhaps it won't be necessary. Have you engaged any new help recently?"

"Indeed, I haven't," and the manager smiled. "I am looking for another salad girl, but it's a real problem to find the right sort of help. I've almost given up trying."

"I can sympathize with you there," Nancy

laughed. "I've been having difficulties of my own. And now I'll not take any more of your time. Thank you for helping me."

She said good-bye to the manager and left the Inn. Driving back to River Heights, she reviewed the conflicting information which she had secured. After all her work had she really made any progress toward solving the mystery of the Crandall jewels? True, she had unearthed a great many clues, but in untangling them might she not lose her bearings in a hopeless maze of detail? Sorely perplexed and a trifle discouraged, Nancy Drew admitted to herself that the mystery of Lilac Inn was likely to prove even more baffling than she had anticipated.

CHAPTER X

An Encounter

Though Nancy Drew had learned little which shed light on the mystery at Lilac Inn, she had no intention of admitting defeat. On the following day she again set out in her blue roadster, visiting a number of the guests who had been dining at the inn at the time of the strange jewelry robbery. Few of the persons were able to furnish information which she did not already have, so on the whole the day was wasted.

The next morning Nancy telephoned the hospital and through the officials learned the names of the two men who had brought in the victims of the automobile accident. Calling upon them, she found nothing to arouse her suspicions. They told a straightforward story, relating that at the time of the crash they had driven to the scene of the accident in their automobile, and when no one seemed to know what to do, had taken it upon themselves to rush the victims to the hospital.

"Oh, dear," Nancy thought, "I seem farther than ever from the real solution. I don't know

what to do next. Unless I find a genuine clue
I'm afraid I'll have to turn the case back to
Dad after all.''

It was no wonder that when Helen Corning,
Nancy's particular chum, dropped in that
afternoon to ask her to go shopping she found
her a trifle depressed.

''You look terribly thoughtful, Nancy,'' she
bantered. ''What's on your mind?''

''Nothing,'' Nancy returned gloomily, ''and
that's the whole trouble.''

''I suppose by that you mean you're head
over heels in another mystery. I know the
symptoms by this time. You always get
thoughtful and crawl into your old clam shell.''

''Why my clam shell?'' Nancy laughed good-
naturedly.

''Because when you're working on a mystery
a fellow can't get a word out of you.''

''Well, I don't mind telling you this time
what I'm working on.''

''What?'' Helen demanded eagerly.

''The Crandall jewelry mystery.''

''Oh, I read all about it in the newspapers!
Poor Emily! I felt so sorry for her. If a
thing like that happened to me I never would
stop talking about my hard luck.''

''Emily doesn't do very much talking.''

''No, she always was the quiet sort. Then, I
suppose she's trying to shield her guardian.

She was devoted to Mrs. Willoughby. Tell me, Nancy, do you think Mrs. Willoughby took the jewels herself?"

"I wish I knew, Helen. I never attempted to solve a more baffling case."

"Haven't you any clues at all?"

"On the contrary, I have too many of them. Everyone accuses everyone else and anyone might be guilty. However, I don't intend to give up until I've recovered the jewels."

"I certainly admire your pluck," Helen said enviously. "I wish I had your brains, too."

"I wish I had the brains you give me credit for. If I did, I could see my way through the terrible maze I'm in now."

"You'll uncover something one of these days."

"I hope so." Nancy frowned. "But the time is so short. Dad told me this morning that the police are getting impatient."

"They haven't learned a thing themselves, have they?"

"Well, they've questioned Mrs. Willoughby closely and have succeeded in frightening her so that she couldn't tell them a straight story to save her life. Dad thinks they will arrest her in a few days if something new doesn't come to light."

"How terrible all of this must be for Emily! She's so sensitive."

"Yes, and I think she trusts Mrs. Willoughby implicitly. She's sort of depending upon me to straighten everything out."

"You'll do it too," Helen returned confidently.

"Oh, Helen, I'm up against it! To tell you the truth, I haven't the slightest idea who took that jewelry. I've investigated every clue and I'm just as far from the solution now as I was at the start."

"You'll find a way out of the tangle," Helen observed.

"I wonder if I shall."

"You're letting this thing get the best of you, Nancy. Why not forget it all for the afternoon and go shopping with me? Your mind may work more clearly after a little recreation."

"Perhaps you're right. At all events, my mind isn't functioning at all now, so I'll go."

"Fine! My runabout is outside. Get your hat and come on."

Nancy Drew jumped up from the window seat and quickly found her hat. A few minutes later the two girls were driving down the boulevard toward the main part of the city. Helen drove skillfully, and to her elation found a parking place just in front of her favorite department store.

"I have a long list of things I want to buy,"

Helen informed Nancy, as the two girls entered the store. "I'm invited to a week-end party and I simply haven't a thing to wear."

"The old story," Nancy laughed. "Well, I'll just tag along and watch you shop."

"Aren't you going to buy anything?"

"I'm not in particular need of a thing right now, but I may see something I want as we go along. You lead the way."

"To the glove department then."

Nancy stood quietly by while Helen made her purchase and then accompanied her to the shoe department. After that they went to the ready-made section and then to the millinery department.

"Are you going to buy out the whole store?" Nancy demanded at last.

"It does begin to look that way, doesn't it? I don't usually go on such an orgy, but this is a special occasion. I'm almost through now. There's only one more place I must go."

"Where is that?" and Nancy gave a mock groan.

"To Hidelberg's for a party dress."

Nancy lifted her eyebrows.

"My goodness, but you're getting extravagant, aren't you? How do your parents manage to keep you?"

"I know Hidelberg's is the most expensive

place in town," Helen admitted; "but I told you that for this once I'm splurging. It will never happen again, probably."

"I was only teasing," Nancy laughed.

Arm in arm the two girls left the department store. Just outside the door they met Emily Crandall. The girl was pale and deep circles were under her blue eyes and her face was drawn.

"Oh, Nancy Drew, I'm glad to run into you!" she cried when she saw the two girls emerge from the store door. "Oh, it's just awful! On top of the loss of my jewels and all that means to me, the police are trying to fasten theft on Mrs. Willoughby! It's too terrible! You will do something, won't you, Nancy?"

Nancy promised again to do what she could. She tried to be encouraging, but she felt that her words hardly rang true. Then Emily said good-bye and Nancy and Helen made their way down the street to the exclusive Hidelberg shop.

They entered, and were at once taken in charge by a salesgirl. They were given chairs and after Helen had made her wants known, were treated to a mannequin parade.

"Maybe this place is going to be too expensive, after all," Helen said to her chum when they were not being observed by the salesgirl.

"I'd much rather dash in where the dresses are all on a rack and labeled 'nothing over sixteen ninety-eight.' "

At last Helen Corning found a dress of pale blue chiffon which entirely pleased her. She inquired the price in a timid little voice and was delighted to find that it was not out of reach.

"You wait here while I try it on," she told Nancy. "It won't take me a minute."

After Helen had left, Nancy amused herself by watching the customers who came into the shop. From experience, she had learned that Helen's minutes were usually long ones. Now, as the time passed and her chum did not return, she became a trifle restless and after a few minutes got up from her chair. As she moved toward the window she chanced to glance toward the door and saw a girl enter. Before she could turn aside, they met face to face. To Nancy Drew's surprise, the girl was Mary Mason.

For a moment Nancy was so taken aback that she could only stare, but, recovering quickly, she smiled pleasantly.

"I didn't expect to meet you here," she said graciously.

Mary Mason regarded Nancy with a cold stare. Then, without responding, she gave an impudent toss of her head and turned aside.

"Such insolence!" Nancy thought a trifle angrily. "One would think she was an heiress instead of a kitchen girl! It was lucky I didn't engage her." Nancy Drew's curiosity had been aroused, and as she waited for Helen her eyes followed Mary Mason. "I suppose she works here," she told herself.

To her surprise, she saw the girl address herself to one of the saleswomen, and it was evident by her actions that she intended to purchase a gown.

"There's something queer about that," Nancy thought. "Surely, a girl in her circumstance can't afford to buy dresses at such a place as this!"

She continued to watch, but Mary Mason, becoming aware that Nancy's eyes were upon her, seemed to grow nervous. After a few minutes she left the store without having made a purchase.

"I'm sure she intended to buy a dress, but she knew I was watching her," Nancy reasoned.

Just at that moment Helen emerged from the dressing room and came over to where Nancy was standing.

"I'm sorry to have kept you waiting so long, but——"

Nancy cut her short by clutching her by the arm.

"Come to the window!" she commanded.

Wonderingly, Helen obeyed.

"See that girl," Nancy pointed toward Mary Mason who was crossing the street. "Did you ever see her before?"

"Why, her face does look familiar. Let me see—oh, now I remember! She applied at our house for work in the kitchen."

"You didn't hire her?"

"No. We didn't like her looks and the position had already been filled."

"She must have called at your house after she left mine," Nancy said. "I'd like to know if she finally found a place."

"I shouldn't be surprised, Nancy. She asked me if I knew of a place and I suggested that she might find work at Lilac Inn. They're nearly always looking for help there."

"Lilac Inn?" Nancy demanded thoughtfully.

"Yes. I don't know whether she went or not."

"I'll make it my business to find out."

"Why, what's it all about, anyway?"

Nancy Drew ignored the question, asking one of her own.

"Tell me, do you remember what day it was this girl called at your home?"

"Oh, dear, it was several days ago. I don't believe I can remember."

"It wasn't the day of the robbery, was it?"

"Why, I believe it was, Nancy. I recall now

that I read the account in the paper that evening." She studied Nancy curiously. "Gracious, you surely don't believe this girl had any connection with the robbery, do you? It doesn't seem to me she would have the brains to get away with it."

"Probably not," Nancy agreed. "But the clue is worth investigating."

"I don't see that you have a thing to go on."

"I haven't," Nancy admitted.

"What makes you suspicious?"

Nancy Drew glanced quickly about to see that there was no one standing near by and lowered her voice.

"Doesn't it strike you as odd that a girl in Mary Mason's position can afford to buy gowns at Hidelberg's?"

"Yes, it does," Helen agreed promptly. "Where do you suppose she got the money?"

"That's just what I intend to find out!"

With that, Nancy Drew dropped the subject and no amount of coaxing would induce her to bring it up again, though to herself she said:

"Oh, dear, one more vague clue to clutter up my mind and to make more difficult the following of any trail."

CHAPTER XI

A Trip to the Inn

After leaving the Hidelberg shop, Helen Corning drove Nancy Drew home in her runabout. She declined an invitation to remain for dinner.

"It's getting late and I really can't stop," she said. "I'll see you again in a few days."

"If you should hear anything about Mary Mason, I wish you'd let me know."

"I certainly will, Nancy; but I imagine you can find her at Lilac Inn. She probably found work there."

Helen said good-bye and with a wave of her hand drove away, leaving her chum standing at the curb. As Nancy Drew walked toward the house she reviewed the events of the afternoon. The more she considered Mary Mason's peculiar actions, the more puzzled she became. Where had the girl secured money? When she had called at the Drew household seeking work, she had been rather shabbily dressed, but at the store Nancy had noticed that she was wearing an expensive gown.

"Of course, it's possible she found work,"
she reasoned; "but even if she did, it's not
likely her wages would be enough to permit
her to buy dresses at Hidelberg's. I can't
understand it at all. Probably I'm doing
Mary Mason an injustice," she told herself;
"but I feel I owe it to Emily to investigate
every clue. I wish there were fewer or that
a few of them were clearer."

Nancy paused on the veranda and glanced
at her wrist watch. It was after five o'clock
and she could hear Mrs. Carter bustling about
in the kitchen preparing dinner.

"I'll have time to run out to Lilac Inn if I
hurry," she decided.

Pausing only long enough to tell Mrs. Carter
that she might be a few minutes late for dinner, she backed her roadster from the garage
and started off down the lake road. Arriving
at the inn, she swept up the driveway and
came to a halt in front of the door. There
were only a few automobiles parked near by,
and Nancy guessed that the scandal of the loss
of the jewelry had already affected the trade.
Entering the inn, she sought the manager and
was conducted to a private office.

"I'm sorry to trouble you again," Nancy
apologized. "But I find I must ask you a few
more questions."

"I'll answer them gladly," the manager returned graciously.

"Have you a girl in your employ by the name of Mary Mason?"

"Mary Mason? No, there is no one here by that name."

"Perhaps she applied for work."

"Not that I can recall. Can you describe her appearance?"

Nancy gave a detailed description of Mary, but when she had finished the manager of the inn shook her head.

"I am certain that she never came here. In fact, if she had, I would have hired her at once, for I am short a girl in the kitchen."

"That's queer," Nancy murmured, half to herself. "Helen told me the girl said she would come here."

"She must have changed her mind. Perhaps she found work at another tea room."

"That's possible," Nancy agreed as she rose to leave. "I'll try to find out."

Driving back toward River Heights a few minutes later, she was ready to admit that the trip to Lilac Inn had been unfruitful. Apparently, she had been unjustly suspicious of Mary Mason, for if the girl had never been employed at the inn, it was ridiculous to attempt to connect her with the robbery.

"Just the same, I'd like to know where she

got that handsome dress she was wearing this afternoon," Nancy thought. "I think I'll try to find out where she is working."

Upon reaching home, she found that she was just in time for dinner. Mrs. Carter had prepared an excellent meal, but Nancy was a trifle preoccupied as she ate. Carson Drew noticed how quiet she was and surmised the reason.

"Not worrying about the Willoughby case, are you, Nancy?" he questioned.

"I'm afraid I am," Nancy admitted reluctantly. "So far, I've not made any headway."

"What seems to be the trouble?"

"I can't get a real clue. I thought perhaps I had one this afternoon, but it didn't amount to that!" Nancy snapped her fingers contemptuously.

"Want me to take charge?"

"N-o," Nancy returned slowly. "I haven't given up yet."

"Mrs. Willoughby came to my office this afternoon. She's beginning to expect results."

"I'm doing my best, Dad."

"I know you are, Nancy. I'm not trying to rush you. Only I'm afraid things are coming to a crisis."

"You mean the police are going to arrest Mrs. Willoughby?"

"I'm afraid of it."

"If I just had a clue—something to start work on!"

"There are some mystery cases that have never been solved," Mr. Drew remarked by way of comfort. "This may be one of them."

"I won't admit defeat!" Nancy retorted, thrusting her chin into the air.

"Let's thrash this thing out together," Mr. Drew said kindly. "Whom are you considering as the possible criminal?"

"Well, there's Mrs. Potter. She was reluctant to give me any information about herself."

"What motive would Mrs. Potter have? I understand that she has plenty of money of her own. She hasn't a grudge against Mrs. Willoughby?"

"Not to my knowledge. Then of course there is that waiter at Lilac Inn—Jennings they call him."

"You questioned him?"

"Yes, and didn't learn anything of value."

"How about the persons who were guests at the inn at the time of the robbery?"

"I've considered them all. The two who took the auto victims to the hospital are out of the picture. They had a perfect alibi."

"And the women who were unwilling to be searched—especially the one who protested loudly?"

"I've not learned anything of much interest about her."

"Wasn't her name Viola Granger?"

"Yes, it was."

"That name strikes me as familiar. I'm sure I've heard it somewhere."

"Can't you remember?" Nancy asked eagerly.

"Let me see—now I have it! That woman has a prison record!"

"A prison record!" Nancy exclaimed. "Are you certain?"

"Yes, the affair happened at least ten years ago, but I have a good memory for names. As I recall, she was sentenced to five years in prison."

"On what charge?"

"Robbery."

"Then you think it was she who took the jewels?"

"The clue may be worth investigating."

"But I don't see how she could have been the one," Nancy declared, with a troubled frown. "She was sitting on the opposite side of the room, a long way from Mrs. Willoughby's table. Several of the guests were willing to swear that she never stirred from her chair, even when the others rushed to the windows."

"H-m, that does seem to explode the theory,

doesn't it? Well, take the tip for what it's worth.''

"I'll see what I can find out about Viola Granger,'' Nancy promised. "But I really don't see that she had the opportunity to take the jewels.''

"Once a thief always a thief, they say, Nancy. Then, with that excitement, can you be sure that your witnesses knew what they were talking about?''

"Perhaps not.''

"After all, Nancy, the police may be right. Suspicion points more strongly to Mrs. Willoughby than to anyone else. She had motive and she had the opportunity.''

"Oh, Dad, don't say that! Poor Emily. Oh, I won't let myself think she's guilty! Emily's a dear, Dad, and that would break her heart, I'm sure.''

After a time Nancy left the dinner table and went to her own room. She tried to write a letter, but found that she could not keep her mind off the Crandall robbery.

"Emily is depending upon me,'' she thought miserably. "I'm beginning to think that I may fail her.''

Over and over she sifted the evidence, but found it impossible to arrive at a conclusion as to the person guilty of the robbery. At last, in sheer disgust, Nancy tumbled into bed.

CHAPTER XII

A New Discovery

THE following morning Nancy Drew's mood of despondency had fallen from her. She rose with new enthusiasm and eagerness to continue her investigations, yet she scarcely knew which way to turn. There were so many clues which needed unraveling and time was short.

The problem was somewhat simplified for her when at breakfast her father volunteered to find out what he could concerning Viola Granger.

"That will save me a lot of trouble," Nancy told him gratefully. "I have another clue I want to work on this morning."

"Anything worth while?"

"I'm afraid not, Dad. It's a cry of desperation, I fear."

"Well, good luck."

"Thanks, I'll need it."

It was Nancy's intention to learn whether or not Mary Mason had found employment, for she had not entirely given up the idea that in some way the girl might be connected with the mysterious disappearance of the Crandall jewels. To be sure, she did not have a particle of evidence to back up her theory except the seemingly sudden access of money, and that, she acknowledged, was too weak a foundation on which to build a theory. Yet, she told herself, she dared not neglect any pointer, no matter how feeble.

She was at a loss to know where to begin her search until she recalled the references which the girl had displayed when applying at the Drew household for work.

"Let me see," Nancy mused. "Unless I'm mixed up on it, I believe she worked for a woman by the name of Stonewell. I'll look in the directory and see if I can find a family listed by that name."

Thumbing through the telephone book, she found several Stonewalls and at length came upon the one she was seeking.

"Mrs. Howard Stonewell," she read aloud, "fifteen hundred and four Sixth Street. I'm sure that was one of the names mentioned in the reference. I'll call her and ask about Mary Mason."

With her hand on the receiver, Nancy hesitated. After a moment's thought she replaced the telephone on the stand, deciding that she could probably secure more satisfactory information by calling in person upon the woman.

Accordingly, she went to the garage for her roadster, and while she was still enthusiastic started on the mission. Nancy Drew was familiar with River Heights and had no difficulty in reaching Sixth Street, which was in the better section of the city. Presently she caught sight of the number for which she was searching, and stopped in front of a well-built brick house.

"Mary Mason must have held a fairly good position," she thought, as she hurried up the walk.

She rang the bell and was admitted by a maid. Nancy asked to see Mrs. Stonewell, declining to state her business. Her confident bearing had its effect upon the servant, who went at once to summon her mistress. She returned almost immediately, saying that Mrs. Stonewell would see her in the drawing room.

"What can I do for you?" Mrs. Stonewell asked pleasantly, as she offered the girl a chair.

"I'm not certain that I have come to the right place," Nancy returned. "You see, I am tracing a girl by the name of Mary Mason——"

"Mary Mason!" the woman exclaimed sharply.

"Yes. Did she work for you?"

"Indeed, she did," Mrs. Stonewell returned dryly. "That is, at one time."

"Then, if you don't mind, I'd like to ask you a few questions about her."

"Why should I answer them? Is she in trouble?"

"I can't tell you the details of the case, Mrs. Stonewell, but she is under suspicion. You will be doing the law a service if you tell me all you know about her."

"I see, you're a detective," Mrs. Stonewell said, in an awed tone. "I'll tell you everything I know about her—which isn't a great deal. She worked for me five or six months ago. I kept her for a month and let her go."

"A month?" Nancy questioned, in surprise. She recalled that in the reference Mary Mason had displayed it was stated that the girl had been employed by Mrs. Stonewell for more than a year.

"Yes, she did not prove satisfactory. I really hated to discharge her, for she came from a very poor family and no doubt needed the money. Still, I couldn't put up with her insolent manners."

"You gave her a good recommendation, I think."

"Indeed, I didn't."

"That's odd," Nancy commented. "Mary

Mason applied at my home for work, and I remember that she showed me a recommendation from you.''

"Then it was forged.''

"Have you any idea where this girl is working now?''

"She changes positions so often that I've given up keeping track of her. However, I do know that up until yesterday she was out of work. I happened to meet her on the street and asked her. After turning her away without a recommendation, my conscience troubled me and I made up my mind that when I met her again I would make it a point to find out if she were in need.''

"You offered her money?''

"No, I didn't," Mrs. Stonewell admitted. "From her clothing it was apparent that she was well provided with funds. In fact, I was amazed. I am sure her family can't provide her with luxury.''

"Have you any idea where I can find her at present?''

"I'm afraid I can't tell you where she lives. I remember she used to visit a brother of hers who resided in Dockville, but whether or not she is living with him, I can't say.''

"Dockville? Isn't that up the river?''

"Yes, about three miles from here. It's a very disreputable section.''

"There's one more question I'd like to ask," Nancy said, as she rose to depart. "While this girl was working for you, did you ever miss anything?"

"No, I can't say that I did. That is, nothing of value. I suspect that she frequently took food from the kitchen, but that is an old trick of unreliable help, you know."

Nancy thanked Mrs. Stonewell for the information and took her departure. When she stepped upon the running board of her roadster she was undecided what to do next. Should she drop the search for Mary Mason or chance an unsuccessful trip to Dockville?

"To Dockville it is," she determined.

As Nancy Drew shifted gears she told herself that in all probability she would waste the entire morning on a wild goose chase. She knew that it was unwise to devote so much time to Mary Mason when she did not have an iota of proof that the girl was connected with the mystery of Lilac Inn, and yet for the life of her she could not force herself to return home. Until she had talked with Mary she would never feel satisfied.

Nancy drove toward the river, zigzagging her way from one street to another. The pavement was poor, and as she approached the slum district it became even more bumpy.

"I'd hate to get a puncture," she thought anxiously.

At length she reached the district known as Dockville, and, at a loss to know how to proceed, made a complete circle of the section. She was confronted with row upon row of tenement houses, all alike and of a dingy and uninviting appearance. Swarms of dirty children were playing in the streets, making it necessary for Nancy to watch her driving closely.

"I'll never be able to locate Mary Mason here," she thought in dismay. "I never dreamed so many people could crowd into one section."

After driving a few blocks, she stopped her roadster and inquired of a foreign woman where she could find a family by the name of Mason. The woman shook her head without replying, and Nancy knew that she had not even understood the question. Going on a little further she stopped at a drug store, but the druggist was unable to help her. At random she questioned persons on the streets, but no one had heard of Mary Mason.

"I guess it's hopeless," Nancy thought in disappointment. "This is worse than hunting for a needle in a haystack."

Nancy was convinced that the trip to Dock-

ville had been a wasted one, but because it was
not her nature to give up easily, she was unwilling to return home without at least one
more effort. Without considering where she
was going, she turned into a winding narrow
street which led along the river front.

She drove slowly, studying the houses critically, though she had little hope of finding
the one for which she was searching. For all
she knew, she might have passed it unwittingly.

The dwellings on this street were even more
squalid and dingy than the tenements, and
were set back a considerable distance from the
road. Apparently, many of the buildings had
been deserted, for windows were broken out,
roofs sagged, and the yards were choked with
weeds. Nancy knew that only the most poverty-stricken lived along the docks. There
were few persons to be seen in the vicinity,
and those she did pass stared at her so hard
and were so disreputable in appearance that
she hesitated to question them.

"I'm sure Mary Mason wouldn't live in a
section like this," Nancy decided.

Without warning she came to a dead-end
street which brought her to an abrupt halt.
She managed to turn in the narrow roadway
and was just ready to shift into forward gear
when she caught her breath in surprise.

Directly across the street, walking toward her, she saw a well-dressed young girl. There was something familiar about the figure and Nancy studied the girl intently, taking care to keep hidden behind the steering wheel. At first she could not believe her eyes, and then she realized that at last her search had been rewarded. The girl was Mary Mason.

CHAPTER XIII

A Surprise

"Can it be that Mary Mason lives in this neighborhood?" Nancy Drew asked herself in surprise.

There could be no question as to the identity of the girl, for she was now close enough for Nancy to see her face distinctly. She wore a neat silk frock, simple in line but unmistakably new and expensive.

Nancy's first inclination was to call to her, but upon second thought she decided that such a course would be foolish. It was doubtful that the girl would tell her anything she wanted to know, and by waiting and watching she might learn something to her advantage. Accordingly, she crouched lower behind the steering wheel of her roadster, hoping that she would not be observed.

Unaware that she was being watched, Mary Mason continued down the street, swaggering a trifle as she walked. Nancy saw her turn in at a dilapidated old house. She paused on the porch, fumbled in her bag for a key, then unlocked the door and entered.

"That's where she lives, all right," Nancy Drew decided as the door closed behind the girl. "Lucky for me that I came this way."

It was with considerable misgiving that she surveyed the house. From the road the place appeared deserted.

"There's something mighty strange about that girl's actions," she thought. "Surely, she wouldn't live in a place like this unless she were reduced to the lowest sort of poverty, and her clothing doesn't indicate that."

While Nancy was debating what to do next, she heard the rumble of a delivery auto. Glancing up she was astonished to see it come to a stop in front of the house Mary had entered.

"Taylor's Store," Nancy murmured, reading the red sign on the outside of the delivery wagon. "Why, that's the largest department store in River Heights! I wonder why it's stopping here?"

Evidently the driver was somewhat nonplused at the appearance of the dwelling, for he studied the number a moment, glanced at a paper in his hand, and then scratched his head in a puzzled sort of way.

"I guess this must be the place, all right," Nancy heard him mutter.

He shut off the motor and climbed out of the van. Going around to the back, he unlocked the rear doors and took out a number of packages. They were all sizes and shapes, but one was round like a hat box and another looked as though it might contain a dress or a coat. In all there were seven packages.

"My goodness, those things can't all be for Mary," Nancy told herself. "Surely, she can't afford them."

The driver of the van hurried up the walk to the house and knocked firmly on the door. There was a long wait and it was not until the man had called out impatiently: "Taylor's Delivery!" that the door swung open on its rusty hinges. Nancy saw Mary Mason take the packages. She then closed the door and the driver went back to his wagon. He climbed in, started the engine, and went clattering on down the street.

"I'd like to see the inside of those packages," Nancy told herself, "but I can guess what they contain. It beats me where that girl gets the money for all her finery. Of course she may buy on credit."

She realized that such a possibility might put an entirely different face on the situation. If it were true that Mary had charge accounts at the various stores, her sudden acquisition of elegant clothes could be explained.

"I don't believe a store in town would offer her credit," Nancy reasoned.

She had no intention of permitting the question to go unanswered. Hastily shifting gears, she started after the delivery wagon which had turned the corner and was traveling northward.

"I hope I haven't lost him!" Nancy thought anxiously.

As she turned the corner she caught a glimpse of red far up the street and was certain that it was the Taylor delivery auto. Speeding up, she soon overtook the wagon, but contented herself with following close behind for several blocks.

It was not until both cars were well out of the slum district that the driver stopped. This was the opportunity Nancy had sought. She pulled up behind the delivery wagon and waited until the man had come back from the house where he had delivered a small package.

"Are you the delivery man from Taylor's?" Nancy asked, by way of an opening.

"Sure. Can't you read the sign?" the driver returned carelessly.

Nancy ignored the gibe and gave the man a smile which disarmed him at once.

"What kin I do for you?" he demanded more graciously.

"Have you delivered any packages to a person named Mary Mason?"

"That girl who lives down in Dockville? Sure! I just dropped off seven of 'em there."

"I hope you got your money," Nancy said slyly.

"I sure did," the driver returned, with a broad grin. "Every cent of it! None of these here C.O.D. gals kin slip it over on me."

It was on the tip of Nancy's tongue to ask another question, but the driver climbed into his seat and drove away, leaving her to gaze thoughtfully after the retreating delivery wagon. What she had learned left her more perplexed than before. From what the delivery man had said it was evident that Mary Mason was buying finery from the stores and paying cash. Again the question that had troubled Nancy from the very start loomed up. Where had the girl secured her money?

"It's beginning to look suspicious," Nancy told herself, a trifle grimly. "This may not be the Lilac Inn mystery, but it is a mystery, none the less. I may have two cases on my hands."

She knew that Mary came of a poor family and it was highly improbable that she had relatives who were providing her with funds. The girl had no employment, and, what was even more significant, she did not seem to be interested in finding work. Otherwise, she certainly would have gone to Lilac Inn at Helen Corning's suggestion. Were these clues or were they not?

"I must proceed cautiously," Nancy assured herself. "I might get myself into serious trouble by falsely accusing her of a crime. So far the evidence certainly isn't sufficient to warrant any action."

Nancy had stood so long at the curbing that passersby were beginning to stare at her curiously. Coming back to reality with a start, she stepped into her roadster and after a little hesitation headed for home.

"I don't believe there's any use going back to see Mary to-day," she decided, glancing at her watch. "It's nearly luncheon time and Mrs. Carter will be expecting me. I probably wouldn't gain anything by talking with Mary, anyway. She wouldn't admit a thing. I must think out my line of action carefully before I try to interview her."

As Nancy drove slowly toward home she continued to mull over the facts she had obtained. If only she could correctly interpret the information!

In reviewing everything she knew about Mary, she recalled that when the girl had called at her home to secure work she had appeared earnest enough. Apparently, she had come into her money since that date and had consequently lost her desire for employment.

"The thing that puzzles me is how she happened to get money just about the time of the jewelry robbery," Nancy mused. "Of course there may be no connection, and again there may be. I remember she seemed startled when I mentioned that my father was a criminal lawyer. It seems to me she wouldn't have acted that way if she hadn't been up to something dishonest."

And yet, in all fairness to Mary Mason, Nancy was forced to admit that in her eagerness to find a clue she was getting the cart before the horse. It was true the girl had refused employment at the Drew household, seemingly because she was afraid of Nancy's father, but at that time the Crandall jewels had not been stolen. Perhaps her money had been secured from a previous dishonest deal. If such were the case, Nancy, in trying to pin the Crandall robbery upon her, was following another false clue.

"Oh, it's all a dreadful mess," Nancy thought in despair. "Every day in every way I'm getting in deeper and deeper."

CHAPTER XIV

New Information

It was not until late that evening that Nancy Drew was given an opportunity to tell her father what she had learned at Dockville, for he was detained at the office on a special case and did not come home for dinner.

"Well, Nancy," he said, as he entered the house shortly after ten o'clock, "sorry to be so late, but I think I have some news for you to-night."

Nancy was eager to tell her own story, but she decided to let that wait.

"Something about the mystery?" she inquired hopefully.

"Yes. I learned a few facts which may throw a new light on the affair."

"I hope the tip is *bona fide* this time," Nancy sighed. "I've been trailing false clues so long I'm getting tired of the sport. What did you learn?"

"Well, I promised to find out what I could about Viola Granger. I looked it up at the court house and found that I was correct about her prison record.''

"But of course that doesn't prove that she was the one who took the jewelry."

"No. But she was at the inn at the time of the robbery, and Mrs. Willoughby and her friend mentioned the peculiar way she scrutinized them as they entered the dining room. That all looks suspicious. Then I learned another thing.''

"What was that?''

"Viola Granger appears to have come into considerable money lately. At least I was told in confidence at the bank that she made large deposits during the last week.''

"Do you know the amounts?''

"Yes, I made it a point to find out. On the twelfth she deposited ten thousand dollars in a savings account and on the fourteenth something over five thousand.''

"The twelfth you say. That was only two days after the robbery.''

"Precisely.''

"Oh, dear, this complicates everything,'' Nancy sighed. "Honestly, it seems as though everyone in River Heights is coming into money suddenly.''

"It's a complicated case, Nancy; but really I thought this clue might simplify things a trifle.''

Nancy shook her head.

"It seems to me it only makes it worse than before." She remained silent for a minute and then said slowly: "Dad, doesn't it strike you that if Viola Granger were really guilty she would be afraid to make bank deposits so openly?"

"Yes," Carson Drew admitted. "I thought of that."

"Do the police know about her money?"

"Not to my knowledge. Of course they questioned her perfunctorily along with the others, but I don't believe they learned anything of interest."

"You haven't told them about the bank deposits?"

"No, the president of the bank gave me the information in confidence. I doubt that the police would be interested in the information, anyway. They have concentrated all their efforts into building up a case against Mrs. Willoughby."

"They seem determined to pin the robbery on her whether she's guilty or not. I think they should sift all the facts before trying to decide who committed the crime."

"The case is a little too big for the police," Mr. Drew observed with a smile. "I understand they grilled Mrs. Willoughby for several hours last night."

"How mean! At least—oh, for Emily's sake I hope nothing will come of that!"

"They're trying to wring a confession from her. Persistence like that is all right for hardened criminals, but I'm sure Mrs. Willoughby isn't in that class."

"Do you think she had anything to do with the robbery, Dad?"

"I'm rather inclined to believe she told us the truth that day she called here, Nancy. Unfortunately, Mrs. Willoughby is very excitable and the police confuse her easily. Naturally, that tends to throw suspicion upon her."

"Are you inclined to believe Viola Granger took the jewelry?"

"I'm frank to admit I haven't arrived at a definite theory, Nancy. However, it begins to look as though this Granger woman may have had something to do with it—provided I'm right about Mrs. Willoughby."

"What you've told me about her sort of knocks my own theory into a cocked hat."

"I didn't know you had progressed as far as a theory, Nancy."

"Probably it would be more accurate to use the word suspicion instead of theory. This morning I happened to make a little discovery of my own."

Nancy then proceeded to relate what she had

learned in Dockville concerning Mary Mason. Mr. Drew listened intently until she had finished.

"I must agree that it does look very queer when a poverty-stricken domestic buys expensive gowns from the best stores in town," he said quietly. "Of course that fact alone isn't enough to definitely connect her with this robbery."

"No, but it's a clue, don't you think?"

"Perhaps. It won't do any harm to keep your eye on her."

"I intend to do that, and I want to find out everything I can about her. And Viola Granger may be the guilty person after all."

"I never saw a case which had so many loose ends."

"Nor did I! This afternoon I felt so encouraged. I thought I'd stumbled on to something that had a bearing on the case, and now I'm not so sure."

"Don't get discouraged," Mr. Drew said kindly. "After all, there may be something in what you have discovered. Perhaps Mary Mason herself knows something and someone is paying her to keep silent. There's that angle. You're certain, I presume, that there can be no mistake about her buying all of those expensive clothes?"

"I'm certain that seven boxes were delivered to her, for I saw them with my own eyes. Of course I can't swear as to what was in them or the cost of the articles."

"It might be well to investigate further before making any accusations."

"I don't know how to find out about the dresses—that is, unless I called at the store. Do you imagine they would tell me anything?"

"I'm afraid not. Most stores protect their customers and refuse to give out anything concerning their accounts."

"But you know Mr. Hodge at the Taylor Store, Dad. Isn't he one of the big men there?"

"Manager."

"Why not ask him to trace what Mary Mason really bought and what she paid for the things?"

"That's a rather ticklish undertaking, Nancy."

"You've done favors for Mr. Hodge more than once. He ought to do that much for you."

"He might do it for me, though I'm sure it would not be according to the store's policy."

"Oh, bother their old policy!" Nancy returned impatiently. "He ought to be glad of a chance to help solve the mystery. Will you ask him to-morrow?"

"Yes, if you want me to." Mr. Drew smiled indulgently.

"Oh, Dad, you think it's perfectly silly, don't you?" Nancy demanded, somewhat nettled at her father's smile.

"Not at all," Mr. Drew responded quickly. "I was just thinking how you always managed to get your own way."

"Not always. Will you see Mr. Hodge the first thing in the morning?"

"Yes, and while I'm about it I'll call several of the other leading stores for you."

"Fine!"

"How about the pawnbrokers?"

"The pawnbrokers?" Nancy questioned, not catching her father's idea.

"Yes. If this Mason girl actually took the jewels herself and was not a chance eye witness of the robbery, she'd have to convert them into cash some way. Through the pawnbrokers would probably be the easiest way."

"Of course. It was stupid of me not to think of that myself."

"There are three in River Heights. If you want me to inquire I'll make it my business to drop in to-morrow morning."

"I wish you would! If we can trace the jewelry through a pawnbroker the mystery is as good as solved."

"Yes," and Carson Drew smiled. "But I'm afraid it won't, be that easy."

Nancy, too, realized that only lucky chance could bring the mystery of Lilac Inn to a quick termination. However, she felt that she had taken a step in the right direction and would yet help Emily Crandall regain her fortune.

CHAPTER XV

What Mr. Drew Learned

"What's the idea of having breakfast in the middle of the night?" Mr. Drew asked the question with good-natured gruffness as he yawned sleepily. "Why, look at that clock! It isn't seven o'clock yet."

"I'm sorry," Nancy apologized guiltily as she poured his coffee. "You see, it was this way. I knew you had a big morning ahead of you and I wanted you to get an early start."

"So it would seem, young lady. But, as it happens, I haven't any special case coming up in court to-day."

"Dad, you haven't forgotten what you promised to do for me!"

Carson Drew, who was fond of teasing his daughter, pretended that he did not know what she meant.

"You were to see Mr. Hodge and the pawnbrokers," Nancy reminded him severely. Then she saw the twinkle in her father's eyes. "Oh, you're trying to tease me!"

"I won't forget to see them," Mr. Drew promised soberly.

"And if you should find out anything important, please let me know right away."

"All right, I will."

After her father had left the house, Nancy Drew helped clear away the breakfast dishes and gave a few orders to Mrs. Carter. She then went to her room to straighten up and gather together a few things which needed mending. Bringing her sewing downstairs, she curled up on the davenport and tried to occupy herself with her work. But try as she would, she found it impossible to settle down. Every time the telephone rang she jumped to her feet and ran to answer it.

"Oh, dear," she thought restlessly. "I know Dad won't call for an hour or two, anyway; but I seem to be all on edge. I think I'll run out and see Emily Crandall this morning. It will help kill the time and she'll probably need cheering."

Dropping her sewing, she dashed out into the kitchen to tell Mrs. Carter that she was going for a little drive and would be back in half an hour. The morning air was cool and crisp, and as Nancy drove toward the cottage on the lake she felt refreshed. Walking up the path with a care-free stride, she knocked on the front door. Almost at once it was opened by Emily.

"Oh, Nancy Drew!" the girl cried excitedly. "I'm so glad you came. Do come inside!" Tell me, have you good news?"

Nancy's face clouded. She wished with all her heart that she could give her friend encouragement.

"I haven't anything definite to report yet," she returned quietly; "but I'm hoping to have something soon."

"Oh, Nancy, you must help me! If you can't do it no one can!" Emily's face clouded and she clutched Nancy by the arm. "Everything depends on getting those jewels back. Dick's future and my happiness! And then there's poor Mrs. Willoughby. The police are trying to brand her as a thief. Oh, it's too dreadful!"

"Don't give up hope, Emily. I'm doing everything I can."

"Oh, you've been wonderful, Nancy. I wasn't blaming you for a minute. I know I shouldn't expect you to solve a mystery when the police and professional detectives can't do it."

"I may do it yet!" Nancy said resolutely. "I haven't given up!"

"I'll be your slave forever if you get my jewels back!" Emily promised rashly.

"If I do, I'll not exact such high pay," and Nancy smiled. "By the way, is Mrs. Willoughby here?"

"No, she went to River Heights early this morning. A detective came after her and took her to headquarters for more questioning. I feel so sorry for her! They haven't given her a day's rest since the robbery."

"You think a great deal of her, don't you, Emily?"

"Indeed I do! She's always looked after me like a mother."

"Do you know anything about her finances?"

"Her finances? What do you mean?"

"Well, to put it bluntly, has she ever been in need of money? Recently, I mean."

"Oh, yes. She always worries about debts, though I guess she manages to get them all paid in some way. Mrs. Willoughby craves pretty things, but her income isn't sufficient to meet all her wants, and that's the rub. She buys more than she can pay for." As she spoke Emily glanced anxiously at Nancy and noticing her sober expression, decided that she had told too much. "I hope you don't think Mrs. Willoughby had anything to do with the robbery," she added sharply. "Why, she wouldn't touch a penny of my fortune!"

"I'm sure she wouldn't," Nancy returned soothingly. She could see that Emily was overwrought. "I intend to help her if I can."

"Haven't you any idea who took the jewels, Nancy?"

"Well, I have several ideas; but I'm not sure any one of them is a good one. However, I think I can promise you that I will solve the mystery during the next few days—if I ever solve it."

"If only the police don't arrest Mrs. Willoughby before that time!" and Emily began to pace the floor.

Nancy cheered her friend as best she could. When she left fifteen minutes later, Emily was calm again.

"I just know things will come out all right," she told Nancy bravely, as she accompanied her to the roadster. "You've never failed to solve a mystery yet."

Nancy Drew had stayed longer at the cottage than she had intended, and once on the road she drove rapidly to make up for lost time. Her talk with Emily Crandall had made her more than ever determined to find out what had become of the Crandall jewels. Though she was inclined to believe in Mrs. Willoughby, she was keen enough to realize that the evidence against her was extremely damaging. Unless the evidence soon pointed strongly in some other direction, the police would have Emily's guardian behind the bars.

"Emily would suffer dreadfully from the humiliation," Nancy thought. "And even if she were later proved innocent, it would ruin Mrs. Willoughby's social standing."

Driving up the boulevard she caught a glimpse of her own home and was surprised to see her father's car parked on the driveway.

"Oh, i wonder if he found out anything about Mary Mason?" she asked herself eagerly.

Bringing the roadster to a halt beside her father's sedan, she sprang out and ran toward the house. Carson Drew, who had seen her from the window, met her on the porch.

"Oh, Dad, did you find out anything?" Nancy demanded before he had an opportunity to speak.

Mr. Drew nodded.

"Come into the house," he suggested quietly. "It may not be wise to let the neighbors into all our secrets."

"You're right," Nancy laughed.

She followed her father into the living room and plumped herself down in an easy chair which all but enveloped her in its luxurious depth.

"What did you find out?" she inquired impatiently.

"Well, I saw Mr. Hodge, as you wanted me to. At first he didn't take very kindly to the idea of looking up this Mason girl's account.''

"Don't tell me he refused!"

"No, he finally agreed to tell me what I wanted to know, provided that we keep the information confidential."

"Of course."

"It seems that you were right about the girl's buying clothes."

"I knew I was," Nancy declared triumphantly.

"According to Hodge, she's been buying scads of things lately. Mostly unnecessary articles."

"Did you find out what she paid for them?"

"Yes." Carson Drew took a slip of paper from his pocket and glanced at it. "A hat—fifteen dollars. Dress—forty-nine fifty. Shoes—fifteen. Scarf—five. Belt—two-fifty. Perfume—eight. Pocketbook—ten ninety-eight."

"Imagine paying eight dollars for perfume!" Nancy exclaimed. "And nearly fifty dollars for a dress when she hasn't even a position!"

"The whole thing comes to more than a hundred dollars," Mr. Drew observed, studying the figures.

"And she paid cash?"

"The packages were sent C.O.D., just as you thought. She paid for them when they were delivered."

"Did you call at any of the other stores?"

"Yes, at the River Heights Department Store and at Hidelberg's. They had never heard of her at the River Heights Department Store, but at Hidelberg's I found that she had bought a dress."

"She must have gone back and bought it after I met her there," Nancy said excitedly. "Probably she was afraid I'd see her buy it."

"That might be."

"What did she pay for the dress, Dad?"

"Sixty-five dollars."

"Why, I wouldn't think of spending that much for a dress myself! Where does she get the money? I think it looks mighty suspicious."

"It does look odd," Mr. Drew agreed. "But there's one weak spot in your hypothesis—besides my suggestion of the other day that some one is paying her to keep silent."

"What is that?"

"This Mary Mason may have come into her money in a perfectly honest way. I visited all the pawnbroker shops this morning and I'm sorry to say I didn't find a trace of the Crandall jewels."

"Would you know the jewels if you saw them, Dad?"

"Yes, I am sure I would. I saw them a number of years ago, and I pride myself on having a certain eye for beautiful jewels. Even if they had been removed from their settings, I would recognize them instantly.''

''Did you describe Mary Mason to the pawnbrokers?''

''Yes, I gave them the best description I could. I've never seen the girl myself, but I recalled what you had told me about her. The pawnbrokers were quite certain they had never seen such a person.''

''I was afraid we'd not be able to trace the jewels that easily,'' Nancy sighed.

''If that girl had anything to do with the robbery, she must have gone out of town with the loot. Perhaps we had better put a detective on the case.''

''Oh, don't do that!'' Nancy protested quickly. ''Please let me work this out in my own way. Give me a week or ten days. If I can't get anywhere in that time, then you can call in the regular detectives.''

''Good enough,'' Mr. Drew agreed, ''unless that girl slips through our fingers.''

''I'll see that she doesn't,'' Nancy promised emphatically. ''I believe I'm on a track now that will lead to an arrest before another week is over! Just whose, we can't be sure,'' she added soberly. ''Perhaps Mrs. Potter's, though I confess that seems unlikely. We'd better look further into that, though. Perhaps Mrs. Willoughby's; but I hope not for Emily's sake. She's a good kid, Dad, and it would break her heart if her guardian had done this thing. Perhaps Mary Mason. Perhaps Viola Granger. I haven't yet found out where she went after she left Lilac Inn that day. Perhaps someone we haven't yet suspected."

"Yes, it's complicated. But good luck to you, Nancy. And now you better get a little rest to clear that brain of yours."

CHAPTER XVI

THE STRANGER

NANCY DREW, hoping that she had hit upon a genuine clue at last, determined to lose no time in gathering evidence concerning Mary Mason. Yet, in considering her next move she scarcely knew how to proceed. Probably it would prove futile to question the girl, but she decided to try the method at last.

Deciding not to wait until after luncheon, she hurried out to her roadster. She started the motor, but before she could pull away Mrs. Carter thrust her head out of the front window and called to her.

"Miss Nancy, if you're going down town will you stop at the corner grocery and see why they haven't delivered the things I ordered?"

"All right, I will," Nancy promised, though she would have preferred not to have been detained.

Reaching the neighborhood store, she stopped to do the errand. Upon being assured that the groceries would be delivered immediately, she went back to the roadster.

She was just stepping into it again when her attention was attracted to a man who was walking down the opposite side of the street. Ordinarily, she would not have given a stranger a second glance, but there was something about this man that commanded her attention.

It was not his clothing which held her eyes, though he was dressed in a flashy suit, but rather his entire bearing. The man walked with an exaggerated swagger which unmistakably marked him as a tough.

From where she stood, Nancy Drew could not see the hard facial lines, but quite without realizing it she took note of the man's hooked nose.

Walking rapidly, the stranger continued down the street. Watching him more from curiosity than anything else, Nancy was about to turn away when she saw something white flutter from his pocket.

"Oh! He lost something!" she thought. "Perhaps it's an important letter! I'd better run after him and tell him!"

She dashed across the street and snatched up the bit of white. To her disappointment it was only an old envelope which the stranger had dropped.

"Sold, that time!" Nancy laughed.

She was on the verge of tossing the envelope into the gutter when she noticed that it bore a

name and address written in a cramped hand.
She scanned it carelessly and her eyes opened
wider.

The name was "Mr. B. Mason" and the address was a street in Dockville.

"Mason! I wonder if he can be any relation
to Mary Mason!"

Startled at the thought, she glanced down the
street and was just in time to see the man turn
at the corner.

"I wonder where he's going?" she questioned. "I believe I'll see if I can find out."

Hurrying after the man, she turned the corner and again caught sight of him. Though she
walked as swiftly as she could, she found it
impossible to overtake him.

"I believe he's heading for the interurban
station," she decided.

Nancy had guessed correctly. A moment
later the stranger turned in at the station, disappearing inside the building.

"It will be simple to find out where he's
going," Nancy told herself. "I'll just saunter
inside the station myself and wait until he buys
his ticket."

However, her plans were not destined to be
carried into effect, for at that moment a long,
piercing whistle reached her ears. The people
standing on the platform began to gather up
their packages and baggage, and the stranger,

who had just entered the station, came hurrying out. Obviously, he had not had sufficient time to purchase a ticket.

Nancy began to run. She reached the tracks almost breathless, and dashed across to the platform only an instant before the interurban cars thundered into the station.

"All aboard," the conductor shouted.

The stranger was one of the first to enter the coach.

"Oh, I'd give a nickle to know where he's going," Nancy thought desperately. "I know he didn't have time to buy a ticket."

"All aboard," the conductor called again, glancing inquiringly toward her.

"I feel it in my bones he's some relation to Mary Mason. There wouldn't be more than one Mason family in Dockville," Nancy went on to herself. "If I let him get away I may have passed up a valuable clue."

She came to with a start as she saw that the train was slowly moving out of the station. Forced to a sudden decision, she ran forward and impulsively swung herself upon the last coach. The deed done, she considered her action with a little misgiving.

"What a foolish thing to do!" she accused herself. "I probably won't have enough money to take me where that man is going, and I'll land in some town stranded. Then Dad

will have to come after me and I'll get the
parental ha-ha!''

The train was still moving slowly and Nancy
could have changed her mind, but though she
was not certain that she had done a wise thing,
she had no intention of turning back. Walking
through the train she caught sight of the stranger and slid into a seat directly behind him.
The man picked up a newspaper and fell to
reading.

Peering over his shoulder, Nancy Drew observed that he turned to a page on which there
was a reference to the Willoughby robbery. He
read the item through and then tossed the paper
aside.

Presently, the conductor came into the coach,
taking up tickets. Confronted with a situation
which might prove embarrassing, Nancy Drew
dug down into her pocketbook. By rounding
up all the nickles and dimes, she found that she
had exactly six dollars and eighty-five cents.
Not a great deal, but perhaps it would take her
as far as she wanted to go.

To her relief, the conductor paused beside
the stranger before coming to her. She heard
the man explain that he had not had time to
buy a ticket.

''Where to then?'' the conductor demanded
gruffly.

''Winchester.''

In relief Nancy settled back into her seat. Winchester was a large city some fifty miles from River Heights. She knew she would have enough money to take her there and back easily.

When the conductor came to her she had her cash fare ready and received her ticket without attracting the attention of the man she was following.

"I hope he doesn't discover I'm trailing him," she thought. "If he does, I won't learn a thing."

The man did not pay the slightest attention to her, but stared out of the window with a blank expression. Some time later when the porter called "Winchester" he sprang to his feet and hurried down the aisle to be one of the first out of the coach. Nancy followed as closely as she dared, but nearly lost him in the crowd on the station platform.

To her relief the man did not call a taxi, but set off on foot. Again he walked rapidly, and it was all she could do to keep him in sight.

Nancy Drew had frequently visited Winchester and in general was familiar with the city. She had not walked far until she became aware that the stranger was leading her into the poorer section, a district frequented by pawnbrokers, fences, criminals and down-and-outers. Once the man she was following glanced around, and for a moment Nancy thought that she must have been seen. But as he continued again she decided that she had been mistaken.

She saw the man turn a corner, and hurried faster so as not to lose sight of him. Turning the same corner a moment later she found to her amazement that he had vanished.

"Now where could he have gone so quickly?" she asked herself. "He couldn't have dodged into an alley, for there isn't one close."

The only alternative was that the man had entered one of the pawnbroker shops along the street.

"I'll wait until he comes out," Nancy decided, with a chuckle. "Then, after he's out of sight, I'll go in myself and give the pawnbroker the third degree. Who knows? I may track down those jewels this very afternoon!"

Nancy waited patiently for twenty minutes and then, because she was attracting attention, crossed the street and walked a short distance only to retrace her steps. She waited another fifteen minutes, and still the stranger did not appear.

"I guess I've lost him," Nancy told herself, in disgust. "He probably saw that I was following him and decided to give me the slip. No use waiting any longer."

Because she was not willing to give up easily, she entered several of the pawnbroker shops on the street and inquired if a man answering the description she gave had been seen. Usually her polite question was answered with an indifferent shrug of the shoulders, and at last Nancy decided that she was wasting her time.

"Just the same, I believe that man went into one of those places," she thought, as she slowly made her way back to the interurban station. "If only I had been a trifle more alert I might have found out something important."

Reaching the station, Nancy consulted a time-table and found that a train for River Heights would leave in ten minutes. She bought her ticket and sat down to wait, discouraged at the turn her adventure had taken.

"Well, I don't consider the time wholly wasted, anyway," she defended herself. "I'm more than ever convinced that I'm on a track that will get me somewhere. To-morrow I'll drive to Dockville and see Mary Mason. And if she isn't willing to tell me what I want to know, I'll find a way to make her tell. I must solve that mystery of Lilac Inn!"

CHAPTER XVII

A CRISIS

IT WAS late in the afternoon when Nancy Drew reached River Heights after her unsuccessful trip to Winchester.

Finding her roadster where she had parked it in front of the grocery, she drove directly to her father's office, for she was eager to tell him everything she had learned. As the door to the inner office was open, she walked in without being announced.

"Hello, Nancy," Mr. Drew greeted her. "I'm mighty glad you dropped in. I've been trying to get you all afternoon. Mrs. Carter said she thought you had gone to Dockville."

"I did intend to go there, but something else came up. Did you want to see me about anything special?"

"Yes. I've been called out of town unexpectedly. It's about that Merrill case and I'm afraid I can't put it off. I should get back tomorrow afternoon at the latest."

"When does your train leave?"

"Six forty-five."

"That doesn't give you much time."

"No, but my bag is packed. I have it here and now that I've seen you I'll leave directly from the office. I'm sorry to run off when you're in such a mix-up about that Willoughby case."

"Oh, I'll get along all right," Nancy replied. She decided not to bother her father with the story of her afternoon's adventure.

"I'll help you all I can when I get back," Carson Drew promised, as he tossed a number of unread letters into a pigeonhole and locked the desk. "Things probably won't come to a crisis for several days, anyway."

Glancing at his watch, he arose from his desk and hastily gathered up hat and traveling bag.

"I'll drive you to the station," Nancy offered.

"Fine! I think we'd better leave at once because I want to get a Pullman ticket and I haven't a reservation."

Mr. Drew made a last survey of the room to make sure that he had forgotten nothing. As he turned toward the door, the telephone jangled.

"Hang it all!" he exclaimed impatiently. "It would have to ring when I'm in a hurry!" Dropping the bag, he snatched up the receiver. "Hello? Yes, this is Carson Drew. What's that?"

Nancy recognized the tense quality to her father's voice and glanced at him in startled surprise. She saw by the expression of his face that the telephone message was disturbing.

Carson Drew held the receiver to his ear for what seemed to Nancy at least five minutes. Then he said:

"Thanks, Williams, for tipping me off," and hung up. When he turned to his daughter, his face was grave. "Well, this changes everything," he said quietly.

"What does?"

"Jake Williams just called. He has a way of knowing what goes on at the police station, and when he thinks I'd be interested he passes the information along to me. He just gave me a tip on the Willoughby case. Things have come to a crisis sooner than I expected."

"What do you mean?" Nancy inquired anxiously.

"The police intend to put Mrs. Willoughby under arrest to-morrow morning."

"What evidence have they against her?"

"Purely circumstantial."

"I don't see how they can do it."

"Well, they intend to. Jake tells me the police quizzed her for three hours straight this afternoon, and she admitted that on the day before the robbery she had visited the bank vault where the Crandall jewels were kept.

Then on the following day she drove to the bank with Mrs. Potter and they took the jewels away with them. Naturally, the admission makes it look bad for Mrs. Willoughby.''

''The police think she went to the bank alone to substitute fake jewels for the real ones.''

''Undoubtedly.''

Nancy frowned.

''Even if she did take the jewels, which I hate to believe, that doesn't explain what became of the handbag which disappeared at Lilac Inn.''

''No, it doesn't.''

''Isn't there something we can do to prevent them from arresting her?''

''I'm afraid not unless the mystery can be solved before to-morrow morning. And that's impossible, of course. If I were going to be here to-night I'd see what I could do, but as it is, I'm afraid we'll have to let matters take their course. Unless you want me to call in a detective.''

''Oh, don't do that,'' Nancy pleaded. ''Give me one more day! I made another discovery to-day that I think may have a direct bearing on the case. I'm sure I can work this thing out alone.''

''All right,'' Mr. Drew agreed. ''Do what you can while I'm away and after that, if need be, we can turn the case over to a detective.

I'll have to hurry now or I'll miss my train."

Nancy drove her father to the station, on the way telling him all that she had learned in Winchester. Mr. Drew seemed impressed by the story.

"I think perhaps you're on the right trail," he told her approvingly.

After Mr. Drew's train had pulled out of the station, Nancy walked slowly back to her roadster, more thoughtful than ever. It was nearly seven o'clock, but as the sun did not set until later, it was still light.

"I'll drive over to Dockville right now," she decided impetuously. "If I wait until to-morrow I may miss Mary entirely."

Once her mind was made up, she did not lose a second. In her enthusiasm for the adventure before her, she had cast a casual glance at the sky and had failed to notice the angry black clouds directly overhead. As she drove along she did think that the air was unusually heavy and that it was rapidly growing darker, but she attributed it to the late hour.

Reaching Dockville, Nancy drove toward the house where she had last seen Mary Mason. Approaching the river, she was alarmed to run into a misty fog which made it difficult for her to see where she was going.

At last she made out the Mason house, but wisely stopped half a block down the street to park. Alighting from the car, she glanced up at the sky for the first time and noticed the gathering murkiness.

"I believe there's going to be a storm," she thought uncomfortably.

Glancing toward the west she saw that the sun was setting behind a bank of black clouds. In a very few minutes it would be dark.

Nancy glanced toward the old house and involuntarily shuddered. Though she was not afraid of Mary Mason, she preferred to meet her in broad daylight. The old house, which from the front appeared deserted, was not an inviting place to visit after dark.

Nancy walked swiftly up the street and paused to survey the dilapidated house. Had she not seen Mary enter the building, she would not have believed it possible that such a place was inhabited.

"It's evident the girl doesn't want anyone to know she lives here," Nancy thought.

She was about to go up to the front door when a sudden thought came to her. Walking to the back of the house, she surveyed the yard curiously. It sloped down to the river and Nancy was quick to see a path leading from the house to the water front. Following it, she came to an improvised dock.

"I'm sure this path has been used recently," she reasoned. "Otherwise it would be overgrown with weeds. I wonder who has been landing at this old dock?''

The faint chug-chug of a motorboat caused her to glance out toward the river. Some distance down the stream she saw a high-powered boat cutting through the water and apparently heading for the very spot where she was standing. Quickly, she stepped back into the tall bushes.

"That motorboat is coming toward this very dock!" she told herself excitedly.

Crouching low in the brush which afforded a perfect shield from the river, she waited expectantly. The noise of the motor became louder as the boat approached, and then suddenly the engine was throttled.

Overpowered by curiosity, Nancy cautiously peeped out from her hiding place. She saw that the boat was drifting slowly up toward the dock. There were three persons visible in the craft, two men and a woman. One of the men held the wheel while the other stood ready to leap out and fasten the boat when the dock was reached.

From where she crouched it was impossible for Nancy Drew to see the faces of the three persons. Darkness was fast enveloping the river, but there was still sufficient light for her to make out the figures distinctly. As her eye fell again upon the girl, she gave a little start.

There was something familiar about her. If only she could see her face!

At the risk of being detected, Nancy continued to watch the oncoming motorboat. She heard a grating sound as the craft struck the dock. One of the men leaped out and made fast while the other helped the girl to alight. He said something to her in a low tone, but Nancy could not distinguish the words.

Leaving her two companions to attend to the motorboat, the girl started slowly up the path leading to the house. As she turned toward the tall brush, Nancy saw her face distinctly.

The girl was Mary Mason.

Having made the discovery, Nancy Drew ducked down again into the weeds, fearful lest she be discovered. To her discomfiture, Mary paused not six feet from where she was hiding and glanced back toward the dock.

"Bud, aren't you coming?" she called in a harsh voice. "This is no time for stalling! We've got plenty to do to-night!"

CHAPTER XVIII

During the Storm

In a frenzy of excitement, Nancy Drew crouched in her hiding place. She dared not move, scarcely breathe, lest she agitate the bushes or make a noise which would attract attention to herself. Mary Mason stood with her back to the brush, but so close that Nancy could have reached out and touched her.

As she waited in an agony of suspense, expecting at any moment to be discovered, a dozen questions raced through her mind. Who were Mary's companions and what had they been doing with a luxurious motorboat? What did Mary mean by saying that there was plenty of work yet to be done that evening? It was all very puzzling, but Nancy Drew determined that she would unravel the mystery before she left Dockville.

Her thoughts were rudely interrupted as Mary called again to her friends, more sharply than before:

"Aren't you ever coming?"

"Say, give a fellow a chance for his life, will

you?" came the rejoiner. "We've got to tie up this boat unless you want it to go drifting off down the river!"

Mary muttered something under her breath which Nancy did not catch. However, she waited for the two men.

Presently Nancy heard heavy footsteps on the path and knew that the men were approaching. Though she realized that it was a dangerous thing to do, curiosity overcame her, and she cautiously arose and peeped from her hiding place.

Through the gathering gloom and mist she beheld the two men. The younger, whom Mary had addressed as "Bud," could not have been more than eighteen or nineteen years of age, but his face was that of the hardened criminal. He bore a marked resemblance to Mary, and Nancy correctly judged that they were brother and sister. She had never set eyes upon him before.

"Why, he wasn't the man I followed to Winchester!" she ruminated. "I wonder who that other man could have been!"

Glancing toward the older man who was following Bud up the path, she gave a little start of recognition. It was the stranger with the hooked nose!

"He must be a friend of Bud's and happened

to be carrying his address," she reasoned.
"That's why I thought he may have been
Mary's brother."

In her excitement at the discovery, Nancy unwittingly agitated the leaves of a bush against
which she was leaning. She quickly ducked
down out of sight, but to her horror Mary had
noticed the movement, slight as it was.

"What was that?" she demanded tensely.
"I saw those bushes move."

"Only the wind," Bud answered indifferently. "Don't be such a coward."

"I'm not a coward," Mary retorted hotly.
"But this business we're mixed up in is beginning to give me the jim-jams!"

"Aw, lay off on the fighting," the older man
interposed bluntly. "It's going to storm and
we've got to make our get-away."

"Yes," Mary agreed quickly, "we must collect our things and escape before the river
becomes rough."

"We'll split three ways and settle everything
to-night," Bud added.

"Three ways, eh?" The other man laughed
harshly. "I tell you I'll have more than a third
of the swag!"

"Don't you remember our agreement?"
Mary demanded sharply.

"What do I care for that?" the man snarled
unpleasantly. "I furnished the boat."

"And who took all the risk?" Mary countered angrily. "Answer me that!"

"I'll have two-thirds or I'll send you all to jail!"

"Then you'll go with us."

"Not much I won't! Tom Tozzle knows how to look out for himself!"

"Aw, quit that arguing and come on!" Bud interrupted. "We'll settle this thing in the house."

To Nancy Drew's disappointment, the three walked on up the path and disappeared inside the house. After a few minutes, Nancy came out from her hiding place, trembling with excitement.

"It's evident they're up to some shady business," she told herself, "but of course I don't know whether they had a hand in the Lilac Inn mystery or not. If only I can find out!"

What she was to do next Nancy Drew did not know. It would be dangerous to enter the old house, for if she were discovered she would be entirely at the mercy of her captors. She guessed that the rooms were bare of furniture and that would make the problem of finding a hiding place all but impossible. What should she do?

While Nancy hesitated, the first drop of rain splattered down upon her hand. Glancing up, she saw that black clouds were swirling about overhead.

"There's going to be a terrible storm!" she thought nervously.

Nancy Drew was by nature a brave girl, but as she glanced up at the leaden sky she was more than a little disturbed. Almost in an instant it had grown dark, and the blackness seemed to have a terrifying quality. The air was warm and heavy. An oppressive quiet was broken only by the moan and rush of the river.

Suddenly there was a vivid flash of lightning, followed by a violent clap of thunder. The clouds seemed to open wide, pouring down a torrent of rain.

"Oh!" Nancy gasped, momentarily blinded.

She could not see a foot ahead of her, but she remembered an old shed which she had noticed at the rear of the house. In desperation, she groped her way toward it. A second flash of lightning showed her the way. Reaching the door, she slipped gratefully inside and shook the water from her dress and hair.

"Just my luck the storm had to break at this very minute!" she thought dismally. "I hope it won't last long."

She glanced anxiously toward the house which Mary and her companions had entered. Through the rain she could see a dim light burning in one of the rooms. Probably at this

very moment the three were dividing the loot
they had mentioned.

"I wonder if they meant the Crandall
jewels?" she asked herself.

The thought drove her to action. Another
impatient glance at the sky convinced her that
the storm was likely to last for several hours.
If she waited until the rain ceased, she would
learn nothing.

"I don't mind getting wet," she assured herself grimly.

Nevertheless, as she stepped out into the
pouring rain, a dazzling flash of lightning
caused her to cringe. Resolutely continuing
again, she crept around to the north side of the
house. There, to her relief, she saw a broad
piazza partially sheltered by vines.

Thoroughly soaked, she reached the porch
and tiptoed across to a window which she could
see gleaming in the dark. To her disappointment she found that the blind had been pulled
down and she could not see inside. She could
hear a faint murmur of voices, but it was impossible to distinguish a word. It was tan-
talizing to be so close and yet not to be able to
learn a thing she wanted to know. Frantically,
she glanced about. She must find a way to
enter the house!

Thinking that she might gain admittance

through a cellar window, she started away from the porch. Just at that moment another flash of lightning made everything as bright as day, and in that brief instant of illumination, she saw another window at the east end of the piazza.

Softly retracing her steps, she reached the ledge and listened. She could still hear a low murmur of voices from inside, so it was evident that she had not been seen. Cautiously, she tried the window. At first it offered stubborn resistance, but as she applied more strength it slowly gave, accompanied by an alarming creak.

"I'll be caught if I don't watch out," Nancy thought.

She waited an instant, but as there was no unusual sound from the interior of the house, she raised the window until it was high enough to admit her body. Thrusting head and shoulders through the opening, she peered inside. At first she could see nothing, but in a moment was able to make out several rows of empty shelves along the walls of the room. Evidently, she was looking into an old storeroom.

"Here goes!" Nancy decided rashly.

She swung herself through the opening and was about to lower herself to the floor of the storeroom when she thought of her shoes.

They were soaking wet as well as muddy. If she walked across the floor, she would leave a trail.

"No use to court disaster," she chuckled.

Quickly removing her shoes, she held them in one hand and dropped lightly to the floor below. Creeping to the far wall, she listened. To her satisfaction, she found that she could hear what was being said in the next room. Evidently, the three were engaged in a heated argument.

"I tell you we've got to settle up to-night and get out while the getting is good," she heard Tom Tozzle say.

"Bud and I will never settle on your terms," Mary replied angrily. "You want too much."

Tom made a response which Nancy did not catch, but the next moment she was startled to hear Mary say:

"Oh! What a vivid flash of lightning! That must have come close. I wonder if all the windows are down?"

Nancy glanced guiltily toward the storeroom window. In the excitement of entering the house she had forgotten to close it. Before she could make a move she heard Mary say:

"I can hear water dripping somewhere. I think the storeroom window must be open. Wait a minute and I'll shut it."

Desperately, Nancy glanced about for a hiding place. She was convinced that her own carelessness had trapped her. Had there been time she would have vaulted out the window, but it was too late for that.

Her only hope was an empty packing case. Hastily climbing into it, she flattened herself against the bottom just as Mary Mason opened the door.

CHAPTER XIX

In the Storeroom

Carrying an oil lamp, Mary Mason entered the storeroom, and with only a casual glance about went directly to the window. As she passed the packing box, Nancy held her breath, fearful lest she be discovered.

"I don't remember leaving a window open," the girl muttered to herself. "Why, the floor is sopping wet."

Hearing the words, Nancy was assailed with a new fear. Undoubtedly, in moving about the storeroom her clothes had dripped water, leaving a trail wherever she had gone. If Mary were at all observing she would realize that an intruder had entered the house!

Evidently, the girl was too intent upon closing the window to notice the floor particularly, for Nancy heard her working with the fastening. Before she could accomplish her task a sudden flash of lightning caused her to give a little scream of terror. Recoiling, she dropped the window down so quickly that the glass rattled.

146

"Say, don't make so much noise," an impatient voice called from the next room. "Do you want to have the police down on us?"

"I suppose you want me to be struck by lightning!" Mary retorted crossly.

"Let that window go," Tom Tozzle ordered. "We've got to get away from here."

"I'm coming," the girl responded sullenly.

To Nancy Drew's relief, she left the storeroom without so much as a glance toward the packing box.

"That was a close shave," Nancy assured herself grimly as she climbed from her hiding place. "It was lucky I heard her coming."

Moving softly across the floor, she again took up her position near the door. Already she had heard enough to be convinced that Mary and her friends were mixed up in an underhand scheme, and she intended to learn everything there was to learn. If only Mary would say something which would definitely prove that she had stolen the Crandall jewels or knew something of their disappearance!

Peeping through a tiny crack in the door, she saw the girl seat herself at a table opposite the two men. Tom Tozzle sat facing the storeroom and Nancy could see the calculating, greedy look in his eyes.

"Now Mary, you might as well be reasonable," she heard him say in a wheedling tone.

"It don't get us nowhere to argue. I wouldn't ask for two-thirds if I hadn't earned it."

"That's a good joke!" Mary returned scathingly. "I could have pulled off this job better alone."

"Yeah? And how would you have got rid of the stuff? Just answer me that!"

"I don't see that you've done so well yourself, Tom Tozzle. You wasted a whole day at Winchester and didn't come home with a cent of money."

"I was followed," the man whined. "I'd have been a fool to have gone direct to the pawnshop. I'd have been arrested with the goods."

"Who followed you?" Mary demanded sharply.

"A girl. Never saw her before, but she looked like a detective."

"Afraid of a girl!" Mary returned scornfully. "It was probably your imagination anyway."

"Tom may be right," Bud interposed. "I hear the detectives are getting pretty active— especially that girl of Carson Drew's."

"How I hate her!" Mary spit out vehemently. "She always sticks her nose into business that doesn't concern her. Well, she'd better not come fooling around me!"

"The quicker I get out of this town the safer I'll feel," Bud said uneasily.

"Before we stir from this house we're going to have an understanding about shares," Mary replied firmly. She turned to Tom Tozzle. "What did you do with the jewels you took with you to Winchester?"

"I put 'em back in the secret compartment of the boat. I'd 've pawned 'em, but I was afraid to after that girl followed me."

"Have we enough money to make our getaway?"

"Sure! That last jewel brought a tidy sum. The money we got from it ought to take us a long way from here. Everything's settled except how we're to divide."

"Why worry about that now?" Bud demanded. "As long as most of the jewels haven't been converted into cash——"

"I'll not stir a step until it's definitely understood that we're to share equally!" Mary interrupted angrily. "Why, I'm the one that should have two-thirds and not Tom Tozzle! If it hadn't been for me, you two wouldn't have known about the jewels."

"You sort of stumbled on to 'em accidently yourself," Tom reminded her unpleasantly.

"I wouldn't call it accident. I went to Lilac Inn to ask for work in the kitchen and as I walked past the dining room window I saw Mrs. Willoughby and her friend sitting there.'' Mary chuckled evilly at the recollection. ''I noticed that big handbag of hers lying on the table, and from the way she was acting I knew right off there was something valuable in it.''

At this point, the girl lowered her voice so that it was difficult for Nancy to hear. Determined to find out whether or not Mary was the one who had stolen the jewels, she daringly opened the door a trifle wider. She thought there was no particular danger, for the room was but dimly lighted.

''I was wishing I could get my hands on that bag,'' Mary continued, growing more boastful, ''when suddenly there was a big smash-up down the road. Two automobiles had run together. Someone in the dining room yelled that there had been a bad accident. Everyone got excited and began running around.

''This gave me the chance I wanted. When Mrs. Willoughby turned her back I just reached my hand through the window and took the bag. It was the easiest job I ever pulled.''

''You might have been caught,'' Bud said to her.

''Not Mary Mason! I'm too smart for the police. I just hid behind the lilac bushes until the excitement had died down. It sure was fun to hear Mrs. Willoughby carrying on in the dining room and accusing everyone! When I saw my chance, I slipped away without being seen and walked to River Heights. Neat, wasn't it?"

"It was clever work," Bud admitted.

"Forty thousand dollars' worth of jewels in one haul! Why, that's more than you and Tom Tozzle have brought in together in the last six years. Now we've got enough to put us all on easy street if Tom has gumption enough to convert the jewels into cash."

"I'll get rid of 'em in a few days," the man promised. "Give me time. I can't walk into the first pawnshop I come to and dump forty thousand dollars' worth of jewels on the counter—not unless we all want to land behind the bars. Now if we can get to Birmingham I know a fence there who'll turn the trick for us."

"How far is Birmingham?" Mary demanded.

"Less than a hundred miles. We can make it easy to-night."

"In this storm?"

"Sure!" Tom Tozzle laughed. "I ain't been a riverman for nothing. I know every crook and turn of this old stream. We'd better get started too, 'cause the storm's getting worse every minute."

"Will you agree about the shares?"

Tom Tozzle hesitated and Nancy saw him

study the girl craftily. Evidently he realized that he could not hope to gain his point, for he shrugged his shoulders indifferently.

"Have it your own way."

Nancy decided to wait for no more. She had heard enough to prove that Mary Mason had stolen the Crandall jewels and that her brother and Tom Tozzle were confederates. From their conversation she gathered that they were all seasoned criminals and had engaged in a number of questionable deals.

"This will clear Mrs. Willoughby and every other person who has been under suspicion," she thought with satisfaction. "I must get away from here as quickly as I can and bring the police."

But in planning her escape from the old house, Nancy Drew had waited too long.

In her eagerness to hear everything Mary and her friends were saying, she had opened the storeroom door a trifle farther than she had intended. Now, as she prepared to make her escape, the conference between the three confederates abruptly ended. Bud Mason pushed back his chair and arose.

Alarmed, Nancy shrank back deeper into the shadow. She thought that if she remained motionless she would not be seen, for the oil lamp on the table did not illuminate the corners of the room. Undoubtedly, she would have

escaped detection had not Fate played a most
unkind trick upon her.

At the very instant that Bud Mason turned
his face toward the storeroom door, a vivid
flash of lightning zigzagged across the sky. It
revealed every detail of the room and disclosed
poor Nancy, who crouched on the floor.

"Who's there?" Buddy called sharply.

Panic took possession of Nancy. For a moment she could not move, so great was her
fright. Then, with the speed born of desperation, she bolted for the window. Reaching the
ledge, she swung herself upward, but a rough
hand grasped her from behind.

"Oh, no you don't, young lady!" a harsh
voice hissed into her ear.

Before she could cry out for help, her arms
were caught in a viselike grip and jerked behind her back. A handkerchief was stuffed into
her mouth. She struggled frantically, kicking
viciously at her captor, but it availed her
nothing.

The gag in her mouth choked her and she
began to gasp for breath. Then things went
black before her eyes and she knew no more.

CHAPTER XX

A Prisoner

WHEN Nancy Drew opened her eyes it was to realize that Mary Mason and the two men were bending over her. She was lying on an old couch and the gag had been removed from her mouth so that she could breathe more easily.

"She's coming around," Bud observed in relief, as Nancy regained consciousness. "I thought for a minute I'd strangled her."

"It would have been better for us if you had," Mary said coldly.

"We're in a mess, that's sure," Tom Tozzle agreed, peering intently down upon Nancy. "She's the one that followed me to Winchester."

"And you don't know who she is?" Mary demanded.

"Never set eyes on her until to-day."

"Then I'll tell you. Nancy Drew! The daughter of Carson Drew, the famous criminal lawyer. Does that signify anything to you?"

"She's been listening to everything we said," Tom Tozzle muttered unpleasantly. He bent

down and grasped Nancy roughly by the arm.
"What did you hear? Out with it!"

Nancy knew that it would be useless to pretend she had not overheard the plot, so she boldly defied her captors.

"I heard enough to put you all behind the bars," she informed them daringly.

"Not much you won't!" Mary cried. "After we get through with you, you'll not go snooping into other folk's business again!" She turned to her brother and Tom Tozzle. "We've got to get rid of her. If we let her go she'll tell the police everything she knows and they'll be down on us in a jiffy."

"That's right," Tom agreed. "We'll see that she doesn't get away."

"Not on your life!" Bud put in.

Nancy realized that the situation was desperate. From what she knew of the character of her captors, she did not doubt that they would be merciless in their treatment of her. If only she could think of a way to escape! She must work quickly or it would be too late.

Suddenly she remembered a simple trick which her father had told her was used frequently by detectives. It was an old device, but she thought it might work in this instance. At least it was worth trying.

Half rising from the couch, she riveted her eyes on a spot directly behind her captors and

gave a low cry of mingled surprise and joy.
Thinking that Nancy must have left a helper
outside who had come to her aid, the three confederates wheeled about.

Like a flash, Nancy Drew was up from the
couch. She dashed across the room toward the
door. With a cry of rage, the three were
after her.

"Don't let her get away!" Mary screamed.

Nancy grasped the handle of the door, but at
the same instant Tom Tozzle reached out and
caught her by the arm, giving her wrist a cruel
turn.

"None of your tricks!" he snarled.

"Tie her up before she tries to get away
again," Mary directed.

"I'll get a rope," Bud cried.

He ran into the storeroom and returned a
moment later with a heavy cord. Nancy's hands
were then tied securely behind her and she was
again flung down on the couch.

"I guess you'll not get away this time," Tom
laughed evilly.

As Nancy felt the cord cutting into her flesh,
she realized that her chances of escape were
slim indeed. Tom Tozzle had done his work
far better than had Stumpy Dowd, the rascal
who had once imprisoned her in an abandoned
cottage. Then, by dextrous twisting and
squirming, she had managed to loosen her

bonds, but this time she felt that there was no chance of doing this. The cords would not give an inch, and the slightest movement on her part brought excruciating pain.

"What are we going to do with her?" Bud demanded practically.

"Leave her here and let her starve," Mary suggested cruelly. "It would serve her right for meddling."

"Somebody might find her," Tom objected. "Then she'd be sure to set the police after us."

"That's so," Mary agreed. 'Maybe we'd better take her along in the motorboat."

"She'll be a nuisance," Bud protested.

"We can drop her off at an old cabin I know of," Tom put in. "No one would think of looking there for her."

"How far is it from here?" Mary asked.

"About forty miles."

"Maybe that's as good a place as any," the girl admitted, after a moment's thought.

"Sure it is," Tom urged. "We can leave her there until we decide what to do with her."

"If we play our cards right there ought to be some extra money in this deal," Bud observed slyly. "Old man Drew should come across heavily to save his only daughter."

"My father won't pay you a cent!" Nancy broke in furiously. "He'll track you down and see that you all land in prison!"

"Not much he won't!" Tom sneered. "He'll be only too glad to fork over the cash when we get through with him."

Nancy subsided, for she realized that she only wasted breath by arguing with her captors. How worried her father would be when he learned that she had been kidnapped! She did not doubt that in his anxiety for her safety he would turn over any sum demanded by the conspirators. She felt sick at heart to think that she had brought so much trouble upon her father. If only she had used more caution and had brought the police with her when she visited the Mason house!

"Well, let's be getting out of here," Tom Tozzle said to his two companions. "It's late, and we ought to be on our way."

Mary Mason glanced anxiously out of the window.

"It's storming worse than ever," she announced uneasily. "I don't like to start now."

"We've got to," Bud insisted.

"But the river is so high. I can hear the water pounding against the dock."

"It's going to storm all night," Tom broke in. "It won't do us no good to wait."

"I suppose you're right," Mary gave in reluctantly. "I'll get the things ready."

She went to the kitchen, returning in about

ten minutes with a package which she dropped down on the table.

"There's enough food to last us a couple of days if necessary," she informed her companions.

"Then I guess everything's ready," Tom said with a critical glance about the room. "The motorboat is loaded with gas and is a r'aring to go. She'll ride this storm like a bird."

Now that the time of departure had arrived, Tom Tozzle was in high spirits. The storm held no terrors for the veteran riverman, but rather offered a challenge which he was eager to accept. Mary and Bud Mason did not share his enthusiasm for the adventure.

As Nancy Drew thought of what was in store for her, she shuddered. She knew that it was dangerous to attempt a journey on the river during the storm, and the reckless gleam in Tom Tozzle's eye told her that he would probably prove a foolhardy pilot. Her unpleasant meditation was rudely interrupted as Bud grasped her by the shoulders and pulled her to her feet.

"Hold on there," Tom cried. "We can't take her that way. She'll let out a yell the minute she gets outside."

"Gag her," Mary directed.

"Oh, please don't put that thing in my mouth again," Nancy pleaded. "I promise I won't cry out for help."

"Gag her," the girl repeated coldly, paying not the slightest attention to Nancy's plea.

Tom Tozzle brought out the hateful gag from his pocket, and, in spite of Nancy's vigorous protests, it was jammed down her throat.

"Don't put it in too tight," Bud warned. "We don't want her to pass out on us again."

Tom Tozzle went to the back door and looked out into the storm.

"The coast is clear," he announced. "Not a person in sight. We can make it now."

A heavy shawl was thrown over Nancy and the two men grasped her firmly by the arms. She was half-dragged, half-carried down the steep path which led to the river. Reaching the dock, she was shoved unceremoniously into the motorboat. The others climbed in. Tom started the motor and Bud cast off the rope.

Nancy Drew heard the angry roar of the river as the boat moved slowly away from the dock. The dreadful journey had begun.

CHAPTER XXI

Down the River

It was not until the motorboat was well under way that Nancy Drew received the slightest attention from her captors. Powerless to help herself, she lay where she had fallen in the bottom of the boat.

The shawl, which in a measure had protected her from the storm, had slipped from her head and shoulders, and she was subjected to severe discomfort from the pelting rain. Though Mary, who was well protected by a slicker, stood only a few feet away, she did not make a move to help Nancy. Rather, she seemed to take pleasure in seeing the girl uncomfortable.

Through a blinding wall of rain the motorboat rushed downstream. Tom Tozzle stood grimly at the wheel, his head thrown back in a defiant attitude. The swirling, rushing water beat against the sides of the little craft, occasionally sweeping over the gunwhale.

Though the current was incredibly swift, the riverman applied more power with reck-

less abandonment.   The boat fairly shot
through the water.

"Aren't we going pretty fast?" Bud ventured doubtfully.

Tom laughed derisively.

"I know this old river like a book."

"But we might run into something."

Tom Tozzle made no response, but neither
did he reduce the speed of the boat. For obvious reasons, the conspirators were cruising
without lights save for a small one in the cabin,
and Nancy Drew knew that this added to the
danger of the voyage. She wondered where
the mad race would end. Perhaps in a crash
against a floating tree or log.

It was not until she was thoroughly
drenched by the rain that Bud came over to
where she was lying and helped her to her
feet.

"You may as well be inside," he said gruffly,
shoving her into a tiny cabin.

"Getting mighty thoughtful of our prisoner,
aren't you?" Mary inquired sarcastically, as
she followed the two inside.

"Well, Carson Drew won't pay us a cent if
she dies of pneumonia," he defended himself.
"How about the gag? Hadn't we better take
it out of her mouth?"

"And have her calling out for help when we
pass the first boat? Not much!"

"She's liable to strangle with that thing rammed down her throat. Here, this will do just as well and it'll be a lot more comfortable."

He took a clean handkerchief from his pocket and, folding it several times, tied it across Nancy's mouth. She shot him a grateful glance as he removed the old gag.

"She'll slip that thing off," Mary protested.

It seemed to Nancy that the girl was bent on torturing her as much as possible and was infuriated because her brother was attempting to make her a trifle more comfortable.

"I've tied it good and tight," Bud assured Mary. "Anyway, you can stay here and keep your eye on her. No need to stand out in the rain. Tom and I will keep watch.

The two girls left alone together, Mary faced her prisoner with undisguised hatred.

"Thought you'd be smart, didn't you?" she sneered. "Well, I guess this will teach you a lesson!"

Unable to make a retort, Nancy coldly turned her back, but even this did not stop the girl, for she was bent upon gloating over her victim.

"You're a great detective!" she jeered. "You found out a few things, but a lot of good it will do you. After this experience you'll be glad to give up the snooping business!"

Nancy Drew's eyes flashed fire. Though she was not one to give vent to rage, it seemed to her that if her hands were free she would certainly fly at Mary Mason.

"Wouldn't you give plenty to get your hands on the Crandall jewels?" the girl went on boastfully. "Well, you never will! And you're sitting not six feet from them this minute!"

Nancy's anger flickered away in an instant. She was startled at this information which Mary had dropped unwittingly, but she tried not to betray her interest in what the girl was saying. From her hiding place in the storeroom she had heard Tom Tozzle mention that the jewels had been hidden in a secret compartment of the motorboat. Probably they were now in the very cabin where she was imprisoned. If only Mary Mason would go on and tell her the location of the secret compartment!

However, the girl said no more about the jewels. She realized that already she had told too much.

Involuntarily, Nancy's eyes swept the little cabin. If only she could think of a way to save the Crandall jewels! From the conversation which had taken place inside the old house she knew that some of the stones had already been disposed of through unscrupulous fences and pawnbrokers, but it was certain that the bulk of the Crandall inheritance remained intact.

Mary, studying her victim fixedly, thought she read the girl's mind.

"Don't worry, you'll never get away," she gloated. "What's more, you'll never see those jewels. I was only joking when I said they were hidden in here. Tom has them."

"She's lying," Nancy told herself.

"Five thousand dollars' worth of the jewels have been sold already," Mary went on, "and it won't be hard to get rid of the other diamonds. I intend to live high."

She strutted across the cabin and preened before a mirror, smoothing out a wrinkle from the silk dress which she wore. In disgust, Nancy again turned her back.

After a few minutes, Mary sat down in a chair and tried to interest herself in an old paper which she found on the table. After reading less than a column, she tossed it down impatiently and went to the window.

Nancy thought that the storm must be steadily increasing in violence, for the motor-boat was pitching and tossing on the water like a wild thing. Mary opened the window for an instant, and a sheet of rain and flying skud came through the aperture.

"This is terrible!" the girl muttered.

After pacing up and down the cabin, she again seated herself. Nancy noticed that the color had faded from her face, and guessed the reason.

Presently, Mary buried her head in her hands and gave a little shiver of revulsion.

"O-oh, I'm getting sick!"

Nancy had not been disturbed by the rocking motion of the boat. Though she had made many voyages, including one ocean trip, she had never been seasick in her life. Nevertheless, she was far from comfortable as she sat in the stuffy little cabin. Her clothing, which was thoroughly wet, clung tightly to her body and the gag bothered her a great deal.

As Mary's discomfort increased, she began to carry on a great deal. Finally, she slumped down on an old cot at one end of the cabin and, save for an occasional groan, remained quiet.

"Now is my chance!" Nancy told herself grimly.

Taking care not to make a sound which might arouse the girl, she wriggled about in her chair and tried to free her hands from the cords. In vain she struggled. It was impossible to loosen her bonds. At last she gave up in despair.

Even more than before, she realized the hopelessness of her situation. Should anything happen to the motorboat, she was entirely at the mercy of her captors, and from the indications, they would not care what became of her anyway.

While Nancy Drew was occupied with unpleasant meditation, Bud Mason came staggering into the cabin. He gave a little groan and sank down into the nearest chair. Mary stirred on the cot and glanced up at him.

"What's the matter?" she asked listlessly.

"Can't you see? I'm seasick."

"I wish this old tub would stop rocking. I'm about under myself. Why doesn't Tom tie up?"

"That old seahorse? He likes this kind of weather."

"Tell him we've got to tie up. I can't stand this rocking much longer."

"I'll see what he has to say," Bud mumbled, and went out of the cabin.

Above the roar of the storm, Nancy caught the sound of angry voices and knew that the two men were arguing. Evidently, Tom Tozzle was unwilling to halt.

This Bud confirmed when he returned to the cabin a few minutes later.

"Well, what did he say?" Mary demanded impatiently.

"Nothing doing. He says we're going to get a hundred miles down the river before we stop."

"I wish he'd get sick—the stubborn fool!" Mary flared indignantly. "Who does he think is running this affair, anyway?"

"Well, he's running the boat, at least. I wouldn't want the job of trying it."

As Bud finished speaking, the motorboat gave a sudden swerve which sent him reeling against the table.

"We nearly struck something that time!" he cried excitedly.

Rushing to the window, he looked out into the storm and was just in time to see a large yacht steam by.

"We might have been run down!" he exclaimed. "This settles it! I'll make Tom tie up for the night!"

He strode from the cabin, to return presently with the news that the riverman had agreed to turn toward shore.

"Running so close to that other boat gave him a good scare," he informed his sister triumphantly. "He says he's willing to tie up for the night now."

"Good enough!" Mary replied. "I'm glad he's coming to his senses. There's no use risking our lives trying to get away when the police aren't on our trail. We can go on again in the morning when the river isn't on the rampage."

Buttoning his slicker more tightly about him,

Bud Mason again stepped out into the storm.
As he opened the cabin door a cold blast of
wind rattled the window, and Nancy caught
a glimpse of angry waters washing in great
sheets over the decks. She was relieved that
Tom Tozzle had agreed to halt, for it was a
mystery to her how the little boat had managed to keep afloat. Then, too, if they tied up
for the night, there was a possibility that she
might find a means of escape.

Several minutes elapsed, and from the sound
of the motor, Nancy knew that they must be
approaching shore. Mary Mason rose from
the cot and staggered over to the window.

"We're coming up to the dock," she observed, more to herself than for Nancy's benefit. Suddenly she gave a wild scream of terror.
"There's a yacht bearing right down on us!
Oh, we're going to hit!"

Above the roar and whistle of the wind,
Nancy heard Bud cry out in a hoarse voice:

"About, Tom! About!"

Nancy struggled frantically with her bonds,
but was helpless. Before she had time to cry
out, there came a terrific crash and the sound
of splintering wood! Then Nancy Drew felt
herself hurled headlong across the cabin.

CHAPTER XXII

SINKING

AT THE wheel of the motorboat, Tom Tozzle had failed to realize the danger until it was too late. Not until the bow of a large private yacht suddenly loomed out of the darkness did he attempt to bring the boat about.

As the two boats came together with a sickening crash, it seemed that the smaller craft must split from end to end. Cries of alarm went up from the yacht.

Bud braced himself for the impact, and though his arms were nearly torn from their sockets, managed to hold to the side of the boat. Tom Tozzle fared less fortunately. He was hurled overboard.

For an instant after his companion had been flung into the river, Bud stared stupidly at the black, swirling water, as though unable to comprehend what had happened.

"Tom can't swim a stroke," he muttered.

Nervously, his hands clenched and unclenched, but the current was running swiftly and he lacked the courage to attempt a rescue.

Rather than risk his own life, he would see his friend drown before his eyes. As he stood trembling at the rail, watching the spot where Tom Tozzle had disappeared, a peculiar crackling noise caused him to wheel about.

For the first time he became aware that the boat was listing sharply, and the crackling sound made him think that a fire had started from the engine. In another moment, the flame might reach the gasoline supply! He darted into the cabin.

"Come on, Mary!" he shouted. "We've got to get out of this! The motorboat may blow up! Hurry!"

"Where's Tom?"

"Flung overboard!"

"Didn't you save him?"

"I couldn't—the current's too swift. Come on, or we'll both be blown sky-high!"

Bud grasped his sister by the hand and dragged her toward the door, but she held back.

"The jewels, Bud! We must get them!"

"There isn't time! There may be an explosion, and, anyhow, this boat is listing more every minute!"

"But we can't go without them."

"I tell you we must! The boat that rammed us may belong to the government patrol.

They'd jail us in a minute if we were caught with the loot. Come on!"

Against her will, Mary was dragged to the door. As she looked out and saw that water was washing over the deck, she became panic stricken.

"We'll never make shore," she wailed. "I can't swim a stroke."

"The boat's almost up to the dock. We can jump for it."

Bud glanced back and saw Nancy lying on the floor where she had been flung at the time of the collision. "How about it?" he demanded of his sister. "Shall we cut her loose?"

He groped in his pocket for a knife, but Mary grasped his hand roughly.

"Don't be a fool!"

"But we can't let her drown!"

"Who's to know? The boat will sink before anyone can get to her."

"But——"

"If we set her free she'll tell everything she knows, and that will mean our finish. Come along before it's too late!"

Bud closed the door of the cabin, and Nancy Drew was left to her fate.

In deserting their captive, Mary and Bud Mason assumed that they left her securely bound and gagged; but such was not the case.

When Nancy had been flung to the floor by the crash, the gag across her mouth had loosened. At first she was too stunned to realize what had happened, and it was not until the cabin door closed behind Mary and Bud that she found her voice.

"Help! Help!" she screamed.

There was no answering cry. Cold sweat broke out on Nancy's brow as she realized that there was little hope of a rescue. She could feel the boat listing. At any moment it might plunge beneath the waves. She tugged desperately at the cords which held her a prisoner, and again she raised her voice in the frantic call:

"Help!"

There was a long moment of silence, a moment which to Nancy Drew seemed an eternity. Then, from far away, she head an answering shout.

"Hello, there! What's the matter?"

"Save me! Save me!" Nancy screamed as loudly as she could. "I'm locked up in the cabin!"

From the vicinity of the dock, she heard an excited murmur of voices. Someone shouted:

"Don't let these two persons get away until we find out what's up!"

Though Nancy Drew was fearful lest the motorboat sink before help reached her, she was calm enough to be pleased that Mary and Bud Mason had been apprehended. When it seemed to her that she was surely doomed, the door of the cabin was flung open.

"What's the matter?" a gruff voice demanded. "The door isn't locked and the boat's touching the dock. Why don't you step out?"

"I'm bound!"

At the time of the accident, the cabin light had been extinguished. Someone now lighted a match and there was a chorus of exclamations as Nancy was disclosed on the floor.

"Get her out of here quickly!" one of the men shouted. "This boat will go down any minute."

To Nancy's relief, someone darted over to her and cut the thongs. She sprang to her feet, but her limbs were so numb that she would have fallen had not one of the men grasped her by the arm.

As she was rushed to the door, she thought of the Crandall jewels, but knew that there was no time to stop for them. She was half dragged and half carried along the deck to the span of water which separated the boat from the dock.

"Jump!" one of the men commanded sharply.

Blindly, Nancy jumped. As her feet struck the dock, willing hands reached out to aid her.

The three men who had saved her sprang after her and likewise reached safety.

"Just in time!" someone murmured.

Nancy, still weak from the ordeal through which she had just gone, wheeled about and gazed toward the motorboat. She saw that it was rapidly sinking.

"The Crandall jewels!" she thought miserably. "They'll go to the bottom of the river."

She dared not go back to the cabin, and yet there must be some way to save Emily's inheritance! Frantically, she glanced up and down the dock and then out across the water. As she saw that the yacht was standing-by close to the sinking motorboat, a sudden idea came to her.

Running along the dock until she stood opposite the yacht, she hailed the captain who was at the rail.

"Don't let that motorboat sink!" she cried. "There's a valuable cargo aboard. Can't you use grappling hooks and save it?"

"We'll try it, Miss," came the reassuring response.

Now that Nancy Drew had done all she could to save the Crandall jewels, she recalled what Bud had told his sister about leaving Tom Tozzle to drown. Horrified at such inhumanity, she glanced toward the inky waters, willing, if need be, to attempt a rescue herself.

"I'm afraid it's too late," she told herself.

However, at that moment a cry went up from the crowd which had gathered on the dock. Nancy turned just in time to see two bedraggled men climbing out of the river. She recognized Tom Tozzle instantly and knew that the other man had rescued him.

"I'm glad he was saved," she told herself.

The charitable thought was not of long duration, for the next instant she saw Tom Tozzle tear himself away from the man who was holding him. Heading for a group of old building and sheds near the dock, he ran like one possessed.

"Stop him!" Nancy yelled. "Don't let him get away! He's a thief!"

CHAPTER XXIII

CAPTURED

As NANCY DREW cried out in alarm, several persons broke from the crowd on the dock and ran after Tom Tozzle. They chased him across the road and were rapidly gaining on him when he slipped behind a group of old shacks and vanished.

"Oh, I hope they get him!" Nancy murmured.

Since her rescue from the ill-fated motorboat, events had transpired so quickly that she had not had time to think of Mary Mason and her brother. Her first thought had been to save the Crandall jewels. Now, as she pushed her way through the crowd, she wondered if the two had managed to escape.

It was therefore with relief that she caught a glimpse of them as the light from a lantern fell full upon their faces. They were being questioned by a man who wore a naval officer's uniform.

Nancy guessed from what she had overheard while still a prisoner in the cabin, that they had been captured the moment they leaped from the motorboat. Undoubtedly, her own cries for help had made their hasty departure appear suspicious. She must accost them before they told an improvised story which might gain them release. Eagerly, she pushed forward.

"It may be as you say," she heard the naval officer tell them, "but I can't let you go until the police come."

"The police!" Mary fairly shrieked.

With a vicious jerk of her arm she freed herself from the retaining grasp and broke through the crowd, striking out furiously at those who would have blocked her path. Her action was a signal for Bud to do likewise. Before the astonished officer realized what was going on, he wriggled free and ran in the opposite direction from that Mary had taken.

"Stop them!" Nancy shouted. "They're both thieves! Don't let them get away!"

A few of the persons on the dock made a half-hearted attempt to stop the two, but for the most part they were too astonished to realize what it all meant. Fortunately, the naval officer was quick to recover himself and darted through the crowd after Bud.

Nancy did not stand idle. Quick as a flash, she was after Mary. The girl had the start of her by a dozen yards, but Nancy was an excellent runner, and in this instance she was spurred on by righteous anger.

Mary cast an anxious glance over her shoulder and saw that she was being overtaken. Bending her head low, she increased her speed, throwing every iota of her strength into the mad race for freedom. Nancy ran easily, but she too doubled her efforts.

Mary reached the road, but there she was overtaken. Nancy reached out and grasped her by the shoulder, but the girl managed to squirm away. She darted off again, but a dozen long strides brought Nancy even with her. This time she did not attempt to hold her, but, getting a trifle ahead, tripped her up. As Mary went sprawling on the ground, she emitted a cry of rage.

"I guess the tables are turned this time," Nancy observed dryly.

Mary gave her a glance of hatred and tried to scramble to her feet.

"Oh, no you won't," Nancy said, and promptly sat down on her.

She was not required to maintain such strict vigilance, for just then several men ran up to take charge of the girl.

"What's the idea?" one of them demanded. "Has she stolen something?"

"No, I haven't!" Mary spit out. "Let me go or I'll have you all arrested for this outrage!"

"Keep a close watch on her," Nancy directed calmly. "And will someone please call the police?"

Assured that there was no danger of Mary's making another break for freedom, she hurried to the dock to find out what had become of Bud. To her relief, she saw that the naval officer had collared him and was dragging him back by main force.

"We have them all now except Tom Tozzle!" Nancy exclaimed.

"They've caught him too," someone in the crowd observed.

A moment later two men came up with the riverman in custody. From his battered appearance it was obvious that there had been a scuffle and that he had not fared particularly well.

"The fellow's a tough customer," one of the men who had captured him observed. "We cornered him in a shed."

"Have you charges to prefer against these three persons?" the naval officer questioned, turning politely to Nancy.

"Indeed, I have! They are criminals of the worst sort. First they stole forty thousand

dollars' worth of jewels from a friend of mine
and——"

"It's a lie! All a lie!" Mary Mason broke in.

"And I happen to know that they are wanted
for a number of smaller thefts," Nancy continued, without paying the slightest attention
to the interruption. "Then when I discovered
what they were about, they made me a prisoner
and took me aboard their boat, bound hand
and foot. When we were rammed by the yacht,
they left me to drown."

"That's so." The two men who had rescued
Nancy confirmed this statement. "When we
found her she was tied up all right."

"The motorboat was running without
lights," a quiet voice put in. "Otherwise my
yacht wouldn't have run her down."

Everyone turned and saw that an elderly,
dignified man in uniform had joined the group.
Nancy instantly recognized him as the captain
of the yacht.

"This is Captain Dudley," the naval officer
said by way of introduction. "There isn't a
more careful man on the river. You can de-
pend on his word."

For the benefit of Captain Dudley, Nancy repeated her story, but when she had finished,
Mary Mason again denied the accusations
made against her.

"It's all a trumped-up story," she repeated. "It's true she was tied up and gagged, but for a very good reason. We caught her trying to steal our jewels!"

"That's right!" Bud agreed quickly.

Nancy Drew was aghast at the statement. For a moment she was so taken aback that she could not say a word, and Mary was quick to press her advantage.

"It's only her word against the three of us," she declared boldly. "Let her prove her story if she can."

Captain Dudley glanced at Nancy with troubled eyes.

"Can you do that?" he asked.

"Certainly I can if you give me time," Nancy announced quietly. "I am sure the police will have a record——"

"Time!" Mary fairly screamed. "She wants time so she can get away!"

"Be calm, please," the captain ordered. "We'll thrash this thing out."

"If her story is true, let her produce the jewels she claims we stole!" Mary continued.

She cast a triumphant glance at Nancy, feeling that she had scored heavily.

"I'm afraid I can't do that," Nancy admitted reluctantly. "The jewels were in the motorboat, and it sank to the bottom of the river."

"That's just an excuse," Mary retorted. "The jewels never were in the boat."

"We'll have a way of proving whether or not your story is true," Captain Dudley said quietly. "As it happens the motorboat isn't on the bottom of the river."

"What?" Mary gasped. For the moment she was completely taken aback.

"Thanks to the timely suggestion of this young lady you are accusing, my men slung grappling hooks into the boat and we managed to keep her afloat."

"Oh, I'm so glad!" Nancy exclaimed in relief.

"All right," Mary said viciously. "Let her find the jewels if she claims they're on board. That's all I've got to say."

"You can do that, Miss——" the captain hesitated as he remembered that he had not heard Nancy's name.

"Drew," she supplied automatically.

"Drew!" Captain Dudley repeated in astonishment. "You're not any relation to Carson Drew, by any chance?"

"He is my father."

"Jove! I know him well!"

He turned to the crowd with decision.

"Gentlemen, I can vouch for this girl. Her father is a famous criminal lawyer in River Heights."

The captain's words had an effect upon the bystanders, and it was obvious that they were again swinging over to Nancy's side. "Call the police," they began to murmur.

"You're not giving us a fair chance," Mary insisted, in her most injured manner. "All we ask is that Nancy Drew produce the jewels."

"Perhaps the matter can be settled more quickly if you do," the captain suggested to Nancy. "Of course you know where to find them."

"Yes," Nancy murmured uncomfortably, "I think so."

She knew by the pleased look that Mary Mason shot her that the girl felt she had won her battle.

"She thinks I shan't be able to find the jewels," she told herself grimly. "And maybe I shan't!"

Though she confidently believed that the Crandall jewels were hidden somewhere inside the cabin of the motorboat, she was not certain that such was the case. Even if they were, she might not be able to find the hidden compartment. If so, she would stand condemned in the eyes of the crowd, and before she could prove the truth of her story, Mary Mason and her companions would manage to slip away.

"I've got to find those jewels!" she told herself. "Everything depends upon it now!"

CHAPTER XXIV

The Search

"Miss Drew, you may as well wait in one of the sheds where you'll be out of the rain," Captain Dudley said, addressing Nancy. "I'll have the motorboat dragged up to the dock where it will be safe to board her. It will take only a few minutes."

"Thank you," Nancy replied quietly.

"Since you're through questioning me, I want to go to a hotel," Mary Mason declared angrily. "My clothes are soaking wet and——"

"If you make the slightest disturbance, we will call the police without waiting for Miss Drew to produce the jewels," the captain told her severely.

"She can't do it!"

"Take the three prisoners into the boathouse," Captain Dudley ordered.

In spite of her protests, Mary was marched along with the others. Though no compulsion was placed upon Nancy, she followed, to get out of the rain which had chilled her to the bone. Her serene expression did not disclose that she was troubled, but in reality she was in far from a comfortable state of mind. Only too well she knew that if she failed to produce the Crandall jewels it would only be a case of her word against that of Mary Mason.

"If I just knew where to hunt!" she told herself anxiously.

She was soberly contemplating the work before her when Captain Dudley came to the door to inform her that the motorboat had been brought to the dock.

"You can go aboard her now," he told her.

"I insist upon being present when the search is made," Mary put in angrily.

"Very well," the captain said, after a brief hesitation. "I'll give you every opportunity to prove your story."

Soberly, Nancy Drew followed the captain to the motorboat, while Mary, guarded by the naval officer, brought up the rear.

"Perhaps I'd better keep all of the bystanders away," the captain suggested to Nancy.

"By all means."

Not without misgiving, she stepped aboard the boat and entered the cabin. Fortunately, everything was as it had been left at the time of the accident, for the rain had extinguished the fire as quickly as it had started. Critically, Nancy Drew surveyed the room, wondering where to begin the search.

"Well, produce the Crandall jewels if you know where they are!" Mary brought out triumphantly.

Nancy did not make a response, but began to open the drawers of the table. As she had half-expected, she found nothing. Undaunted, she made the rounds of the walls, tapping upon them sharply with her knuckles. To her disappointment, there was no indication of a hollow behind any of the panels.

"Didn't I tell you?" Mary demanded of the captain. "Now will you let me go?"

"I'm not through searching yet," Nancy said sharply. "I know the jewels are hidden here somewhere."

"Take all the time you need," Captain Dudley told her kindly.

Again Nancy Drew surveyed the room. She could not admit defeat, and yet she was at her wit's end.

As her eyes roamed over the walls again, her attention was attracted to a round-faced wall clock which had stopped at the hour of twelve. The timepiece was very ordinary in appearance, and Nancy might not have given it as much as a second glance had she not chanced to look toward Mary Mason.

The girl was staring fixedly at the clock and for one fleeting instant there was an expression of stark terror in her smoldering eyes. The next moment she looked away from the wall indifferently, but Nancy Drew was not to be deceived.

She rushed eagerly over to the clock. It was far above her head, but by mounting upon the cot she found that she could reach it.

"Well, of all the silly things!" Mary burst out, but there was a tremor to her voice.

Quickly, Nancy reached up and opened the glass door of the clock. The cardboard face did not appear to be securely in place, and upon impulse she began to pry at it with her fingers.

"Here's my knife," Captain Dudley offered.

"Thank you, that's just what I need."

Nancy took the knife and pried off two tiny screws. The face then dropped down into her hands.

"Oh!" she cried. "The secret compartment! I've found it!"

She had expected to view the "works" of the clock, but instead beheld a round metal box which fit snugly into the wall. The clock was only a clever sham. To her delight, she found that the metal box could be removed from the wall.

Placing it on the table, Nancy surveyed Mary Mason triumphantly.

"I guess this proves my story, doesn't it?"

She fumbled with the catch on the box and lifted the lid. There before her was an array of jewels such as she had never viewed before in her life. Brilliant diamonds mounted in old-fashioned rings and quaint bracelets. Pendants of rubies and broaches of sapphires. For a moment, Nancy Drew was so dazzled by the display that she could only stare open-mouthed.

"My word!" Captain Dudley exclaimed, breaking the silence. "What a collection!"

"They belong to Emily Crandall, a friend of mine," Nancy explained. "I'm afraid some of the jewels are missing."

Captain Dudley turned sternly upon Mary.

"What have you to say for yourself now, young lady?"

Mary's arrogant air had fallen completely from her. She looked crushed and beaten.

"Well, I guess you have the goods on me," she admitted with a shrug of her shoulders.

"Do you admit that Miss Drew's story is true?"

"Yes, I stole the jewels."

"What have you done with the ones that are missing?" Nancy broke in.

"Out with it!" Captain Dudley commanded sharply. "It will go harder with you if you try to keep anything back."

"We pawned several of the diamonds," Mary admitted grudgingly.

"Where?" Nancy demanded.

"At a pawnshop Tom Tozzle knows about in

Winchester. It's a place on Bond Street.''

"I know the locality,'' Nancy told the captain. "It's possible that we'll be able to recover the jewels. I believe it's a law that pawnbrokers must not accept stolen goods.''

"The first thing to do is to land our prisoners in jail,'' the captain suggested. "If you'll take charge of the jewels, Miss Drew, I'll step out and call the police.''

Within fifteen minutes the authorities had arrived at the dock and the three prisoners were handcuffed and hustled into the patrol wagon.

"We've been on the watch for this jane nearly a year,'' one of the policemen told Nancy. "She's wanted for half a dozen smaller thefts. You've done a good night's work, young lady.''

"I live in River Heights,'' Nancy returned, with a smile. "If you need me to testify, I'll be at your service.''

After the patrol wagon had departed, the crowd began to disperse. For the first time Nancy Drew realized that the hour was late.

"Why, it's after four o'clock,'' she said in astonishment, as she glanced at her wrist watch.

"Won't you do me the honor of taking breakfast at my home?'' Captain Dudley asked. "My wife will be delighted.''

"At this hour?" Nancy laughed. She shook her head. "No, I must get back to River Heights just as quickly as I can. Poor Mrs. Willoughby is under suspicion for the theft of the Crandall jewels and the police intend to arrest her."

"Then of course I won't try to hold you here. When you see your father, give him my kindest regards."

"I will," Nancy promised. "And now, if someone will tell me where I can get a taxi-cab——"

"I'll be glad to drive you to River Heights in my car," the naval officer volunteered. "If you intend to take those jewels with you, you'll need someone to go along as a guard."

"Perhaps you are right. I shall be delighted to accept your kind offer."

During the night the storm had blown itself out, and as Nancy Drew stepped into the automobile she noticed that the sky had cleared. Gazing toward the east, she was surprised to see that the sun was about to peep over the horizon.

"Ho-hum," she yawned sleepily. "It's been a terrible night, but I wouldn't have missed it for anything! I only hope I get home safely with these jewels. As soon as I deliver them, I'm going to bed and sleep a month!"

CHAPTER XXV

NANCY'S REWARD

EVEN to the casual wayfarer who chanced to pass Lilac Inn on a certain evening late in July, it must have been apparent that an unusual affair was in progress. The inn was aglow with gay, twinkling lights and the grounds were as brightly illuminated as though it were day. Colored searchlights played over the rippling waters of the lake. From the largest of the private dining rooms came the soft, blended notes of cello, violin, and harp.

Grouped about a long table sat many distinguished-looking men and women, but as they chatted together one would have noticed that their eyes frequently turned toward a young girl who occupied the seat of honor. Indeed, Nancy Drew had never appeared more lovely than on this evening when she occupied the limelight.

"Oh, Mrs. Willoughby, it's the grandest party I ever attended," she sighed dreamily, addressing her hostess. "It was perfectly marvelous of you and Emily to give it for me. I don't deserve it at all."

"Hear! Hear!" several of the guests laughed.

"My dear Nancy," Mrs. Willoughby said, with a bright smile. "I owe you more than I can ever repay. Why, if it hadn't been for you, I would probably be in jail at this very minute," and she shuddered a bit.

"Surely, not as bad as that," Carson Drew remarked lightly. "They couldn't have held you on such flimsy evidence."

"But I would have been arrested," Mrs. Willoughby insisted, "and that would have been dreadfully mortifying. Nancy saved me a great deal of embarrassment."

"She saved more than that for me," Emily Crandall broke in. "I'd never have seen my jewels again if she hadn't found them for me."

"Did you finally recover them all?" Mrs. Potter questioned, with interest. "I thought part of them had been pawned."

"Nancy got them all back for me," Emily declared proudly. "That is, all but about three hundred dollars' worth, and I can afford to lose that much. You see, she traced them to a pawnbroker in Winchester and had him arrested for accepting stolen goods. He was forced to give everything back."

"It really wasn't hard to trace the jewels," Nancy observed quietly.

"I guess nothing is very hard for you," Mrs. Willoughby laughed. "Really you seem to have a genius for solving mysteries."

"Speaking of mysteries," Carson Drew broke in. "Mrs. Willoughby has never explained to us why she went to the bank vault on the day before she planned to deliver the jewels."

"It was silly of me, wasn't it? And it made the police so suspicious! Well, to tell the truth, I was worried about Emily's jewels, and I wanted to make certain that they were safe in the vault. Of course I knew they would be there but, well, I guess I'm the nervous sort. The police wouldn't believe me when I told them. Under the circumstance, I suppose it was natural for them to suspect me."

"The fact that you were known to be in hard circumstance made the case look worse, too," Mr. Drew remarked.

"Yes, at that time I thought I might have to borrow money, but fortunately an investment has turned out much better than I expected, so I'm still a woman of means."

"I guess we were all under suspicion," Mrs. Potter observed dryly. "I'm sure Miss Drew considered me as the possible villain."

"Not seriously," Nancy laughed. "Though

you must admit you didn't take kindly to my questions."

"No, I didn't," Mrs. Potter admitted soberly. "And I sincerely apologize for the way I failed to co-operate. You see, at first I thought you were trying to throw suspicion on me and I was afraid to tell you anything."

"And then there was that young woman, Viola Granger," Mr. Drew remarked. "She attracted my attention because of her prison record. I wasn't able to explain her sudden acquisition of money."

"Where did she get it?" Mrs. Willoughby inquired curiously. "I never heard."

"In a perfectly legitimate manner. I have been told she invested in a wild-cat oil scheme and, as luck would have it, they brought in a gusher."

"And poor Jennings!" Emily said reflectively. "We did him an injustice."

"I was positive he was the one who took the handbag," Mrs. Willoughby said regretfully. "However, I've tried to make it up to him by giving him a generous present."

"I'm glad to see that Lilac Inn is doing a thriving business again, too," Mr. Drew remarked. "For a time it looked as though the scandal might ruin the trade."

"The manager certainly has Nancy to thank," Emily said earnestly.

Nancy laughed.

"She's done it already. This afternoon she told me that anytime I wanted to I could come out here for dinner and bring my friends—and it wouldn't cost me a cent!"

"It's mighty nice to have a smart little daughter," Mr. Drew declared, with a twinkle in his eyes. "Reduces the board bill, for one thing."

"Dad, you mercenary creature!"

"Seriously, I am proud of you, Nancy." A tender note crept into the lawyer's voice. "It was a clever piece of detective work. I admit that when you started out, I didn't have much hope that you'd solve the case."

"I was doubtful myself, Dad. Especially when they tied me up and left me on that motorboat to drown."

Mr. Drew shook his head sadly.

"You'll worry me into an early grave with all your wild adventures."

"I hope not, because I intend to have a lot more," Nancy returned gayly. And she did, as you will find in reading of her further adventures in solving mysteries. "After all, I'm only following in your footsteps."

"Well, all's well that ends well. That Mason girl and her confederates are locked up where they'll make no more trouble."

"I didn't hear how the trial came out," Mrs. Potter remarked.

"They admitted their guilt," Mr. Drew returned. "So there wasn't a trial. The judge gave them long sentences. They were wanted for a number of other robberies."

"It's a wonder that girl didn't steal Mrs. Stonewell blind when she worked there," Emily observed.

"Yes," Nancy agreed, "when I learned that she hadn't taken anything, I was thrown off the track a little. I suppose she was planning a big haul and was discharged before she could carry her plans into effect."

"Mrs. Stonewell was lucky to escape without having her whole house carted away."

"She called me on the telephone yesterday and thanked me for being instrumental in Mary's capture. I guess she read the account in the paper."

"I think everyone must have thanked you except me," Emily said soberly.

"Why, Emily Crandall! What do you mean? It seems to me you've thanked me a million times a day ever since I got those jewels back."

"But I mean in a material way. You ought to charge a commission for recovering the jewels. Let me see, ten per cent of forty thousand dollars would be——"

"I don't do business that way," Nancy laughed. "You know very well I won't take a penny of your money."

"Nancy has always made it a point never to accept a money reward," Carson Drew stated, coming to his daughter's aid.

"Oh, dear, I was afraid she wouldn't! And for that reason I came prepared!" As she spoke, Emily brought out a small package and handed it to Nancy with a flourish. "There!" she cried. "Don't you dare refuse to accept it, either!"

"Why, Emily, what are you giving me?" Nancy asked in surprise, as she fumbled at the silver ribbon.

"It's just a souvenir to show you how much I appreciate all you've done for me."

Nancy unwrapped the little package while the others watched eagerly. As the folds of tissue paper fell away she beheld the gift—a beautiful bracelet set with precious stones. It was one of the quaintest pieces in the Crandall collection.

"Oh, Emily!" Nancy gasped in delight. "Oh, how lovely!"

"You can have the jewels reset if you like."

"I wouldn't think of it! I love it the way it is! But, really, I shouldn't take this bracelet, Emily. It represents a great deal of money."

"It's little enough to offer you for everything you've done. You'll keep it, won't you?"

Nancy hesitated and then nodded her head. She saw that Emily would be crushed if she refused the gift. And then, she would have found it difficult to have given back such an exquisite piece of jewelry.

After she had thanked her friend for the gift, someone proposed a toast, and to Nancy's embarrassment, everyone sprang to his feet to give it with a will. At last, however, the party broke up.

Nancy was turning to leave when Emily drew her aside and led her out upon the veranda.

"There's something special I wanted to tell you, but I didn't like to shout it out when the others could hear," she began in a confidential tone of voice. "Dick and I are going to be married next month."

"Oh, I'm so glad, Emily. I wish you all happiness and prosperity."

"Thanks. I want to ask a special favor."

"Go ahead."

"Will you serve as maid of honor at my wedding?"

"Anything you like, Emily. I'll even be ring bearer if you ask it."

"I knew you wouldn't fail me. Oh, it seems as though I have more happiness than I deserve."

Emily gazed out across the lake and gave the

gentle sigh of the love lorn. Nancy squeezed her hand understandingly. She, too, turned to watch the twinkling lights on the water.

"The end of a perfect night," Nancy Drew said softly. "And what could be more fitting than that the mystery of the Crandall jewels should fade out just where it began—at Lilac Inn."

THE END

This Isn't All!

Would you like to know what became of the good friends you have made in this book?

Would you like to read other stories continuing their adventures and experiences, or other books quite as entertaining by the same author?

On the *reverse side* of the wrapper which comes with this book, you will find a wonderful list of stories which you can buy at the same store where you got this book.

Don't throw away the Wrapper

Use it as a handy catalog of the books you want some day to have. But in case you do mislay it, write to the Publishers for a complete catalog.

THE OUTDOOR GIRLS SERIES

by LAURA LEE HOPE
Author of The Blythe Girls Books

Every Volume Complete in Itself.

These are the adventures of a group of bright, fun-loving, up-to-date girls who have a common bond in their fondness for outdoor life, camping, travel and adventure. There is excitement and humor in these stories and girls will find in them the kind of pleasant associations that they seek to create among their own friends and chums.

THE OUTDOOR GIRLS OF DEEPDALE
THE OUTDOOR GIRLS AT RAINBOW LAKE
THE OUTDOOR GIRLS IN A MOTOR CAR
THE OUTDOOR GIRLS IN A WINTER CAMP
THE OUTDOOR GIRLS IN FLORIDA
THE OUTDOOR GIRLS AT OCEAN VIEW
THE OUTDOOR GIRLS IN ARMY SERVICE
THE OUTDOOR GIRLS ON PINE ISLAND
THE OUTDOOR GIRLS AT THE HOSTESS
   HOUSE
THE OUTDOOR GIRLS AT BLUFF POINT
THE OUTDOOR GIRLS AT WILD ROSE
   LODGE
THE OUTDOOR GIRLS IN THE SADDLE
THE OUTDOOR GIRLS AROUND THE
   CAMPFIRE
THE OUTDOOR GIRLS ON CAPE COD
THE OUTDOOR GIRLS AT FOAMING FALLS
THE OUTDOOR GIRLS ALONG THE COAST
THE OUTDOOR GIRLS AT SPRING HILL
   FARM
THE OUTDOOR GIRLS AT NEW MOON
   RANCH
THE OUTDOOR GIRLS ON A HIKE
THE OUTDOOR GIRLS ON A CANOE TRIP

GROSSET & DUNLAP, *Publishers,* **NEW YORK**

THE BLYTHE GIRLS BOOKS

By LAURA LEE HOPE

Author of The Outdoor Girls Series

Illustrated by Thelma Gooch

The Blythe Girls, three in number, were left alone in New York City. Helen, who went in for art and music, kept the little flat uptown, while Margy, just out of business school, obtained a position as secretary and Rose, plain-spoken and business-like, took what she called a "job" in a department store. The experiences of these girls make fascinating reading—life in the great metropolis is thrilling and full of strange adventures and surprises.

THE BLYTHE GIRLS: HELEN, MARGY AND ROSE

THE BLYTHE GIRLS: MARGY'S QUEER INHERITANCE

THE BLYTHE GIRLS: ROSE'S GREAT PROBLEM

THE BLYTHE GIRLS: HELEN'S STRANGE BOARDER

THE BLYTHE GIRLS: THREE ON A VACATION

THE BLYTHE GIRLS: MARGY'S SECRET MISSION

THE BLYTHE GIRLS: ROSE'S ODD DISCOVERY

THE BLYTHE GIRLS: THE DISAPPEARANCE OF HELEN

THE BLYTHE GIRLS: SNOWBOUND IN CAMP

THE BLYTHE GIRLS: MARGY'S MYSTERIOUS VISITOR

GROSSET & DUNLAP *Publishers* NEW YORK